The NEW TESTAMENT for TODAY

D1636792

W. Jeffrey Marsh & Ron R. Munns

BOOKCRAFT

Salt Lake City, Utah

Library of Congress Catalog Card Number: 94-73200
ISBN 0-88494-965-6

First Printing, 1994

Printed in the United States of America

Contents

Introduction

How important are stories in our lives? Crafting our experiences into stories is "the way we make ourselves at home in the world," observed author William Kittredge (see *Hole in the Sky*, p. 29; cited in *Brigham Young Magazine*, February 1994, p. 60).

Stories from the scriptures and from the lives of faithful Saints help us remember who we are and what we have covenanted to do. "Human beings require stories to give meaning to the facts of their existence," affirms Neil Postman. "If our stories are coherent and plausible and have continuity, they will help us to understand why we are here, and what we need to pay attention to and what we may ignore." Stories provide "a structure for our perceptions. . . . Only through stories do facts assume any meaning whatsoever. . . . [We] require a story to give meaning to [our] existence. Without air, our cells die. Without a story, our selves die." (See *Atlantic Monthly*, December 1989; as cited in *Brigham Young Magazine*, February 1994, p. 60.)

The most important stories ever told come from the Savior's life. Beginning with his baptism and culminating with the Resurrection, the Savior's three-and-a-half year ministry presented countless miracles and innumerable blessings. John the Beloved wrote, "And there are also many other things which Jesus did, the which, if they should be written every one, I suppose that even the world itself could not contain the books that should be written" (John 21:25).

The four Gospels are not elaborate, detailed histories of Christ's life. They are witnesses of his authority, and they testify of his power. Of his three-and-a-half year ministry, only the events from about thirty days are recorded in Matthew, Mark, Luke, and John. That's less than one-fourth of one percent! In fact, we do not even have a record of some of the Savior's greatest teachings and miracles. Matthew wrote, "Then began he to upbraid the cities wherein *most of his mighty works were done,* because they repented not: Woe unto thee, Chorazin! woe unto thee, Bethsaida! for if the mighty works, which were done in you, had been done in Tyre and Sidon, they would have repented long ago in sackcloth and ashes." (Matthew 11:20–21; emphasis added.) None of those "mighty works" are recorded in the scriptural records. How grateful we should be for what was written!

All of the Gospel writers bore witness of the Divine Healer with stories. Matthew wrote a moving account of the Master's invitation to a paralytic to "arise and walk." Curiously following this account is Matthew's own calling to the apostleship. (See Matthew 9:2–9.) Could it be that this publican of controversial social status wanted to show the spiritual healing power of Jesus as he too "arose" and walked with Christ?

President Harold B. Lee testified, "The greatest miracles I see today are not necessarily the healing of sick bodies, but the greatest miracles I see are the healing of sick souls, those who are sick in soul and spirit and are downhearted" (in Conference Report, April 1973, p. 178).

Stories of healing and miracles of compassion are a significant part of the Church yesterday and today. Elder Spencer W. Kimball said, "A question often asked is: 'If miracles are a part of the Gospel program, why do we not have such today?'

"The answer is a simple one: We do have miracles today— beyond imagination! If all the miracles of our own lifetime were recorded, it would take many library shelves to hold the books which would contain them.

"What kinds of miracles do we have? All kinds—revelations, visions, tongues, healings, special guidance and direction, evil spirits cast out. Where are they recorded? In the records of the

Church, in journals, in news and magazine articles and in the minds and memories of many people." ("The Significance of Miracles in the Church Today," *Instructor*, December 1959, p. 396.)

"Come unto me," a loving Savior beckons. His invitation has always been the same. He offers lasting peace to those who will accept: "Come unto me, . . . and I will give you rest" (Matthew 11:28). There is no where else to go: "I am the way, the truth, and the life" (John 14:6). Without his example, all would be dark: "I am the light; I have set an example for you" (3 Nephi 18:16; see also verse 24). Without his help we would spiritually starve: "I am [the] bread of life" (John 6:48). Without his friendship we are lost: "And this is life eternal, that they might know thee the only true God, and Jesus Christ, whom thou hast sent" (John 17:3).

Truly, there is no greater story to study than the story of his life, no greater personality to pattern our lives after than his character, no more important lessons to understand than his teachings: "Learn of me; for I am meek and lowly in heart: and ye shall find rest unto your souls" (Matthew 11:29). Become "even as I am," the Savior invites (3 Nephi 27:27), and "be perfected in [me]" (Moroni 10:32).

Jesus' life and teachings motivate us to change. "We know that, when he shall appear, we shall be like him" (1 John 3:2). And this change is real. President David O. McKay said, "What you sincerely in your heart think of Christ will determine what you are, will largely determine what your acts will be. No person can study this divine personality, can accept his teachings without becoming conscious of an uplifting and refining influence within himself. . . . Members of the Church of Christ are under obligation to make the sinless Son of Man their ideal—the one perfect being who ever walked the earth." (In Conference Report, April 1951, pp. 93, 98.)

President Ezra Taft Benson added, "The Lord works from the inside out. The world works from the outside in. The world would take people out of the slums. Christ takes the slums out of people, and then they take themselves out of the slums. The world would mold men by changing their environment. Christ changes men, who then change their environment. The world would shape human behavior, but Christ can change human nature." ("Born of God," *Ensign*, November 1985, p. 5.)

The stories told about the Savior in the scriptures have the seal of living reality put on them when we read of similar, contemporary experiences. Modern miracles and blessings witness to all that God is the same yesterday, today, and forever. And that message is the heart of the restored gospel of Jesus Christ.

As you read these marvelous experiences, ask yourself, "Would God do that for me? Has that ever happened to me or someone close to me?" Try to find similar stories in your own life. Such stories bear an even greater witness that God works today as he did in times of old. If God works miracles in our lives today, does it not bear witness that he cares for us just as much as he loved those people in the scriptures? We are all of great worth to him. His "work and glory" is indeed to bring to pass our eternal life (see Moses 1:39).

May the choicest miracles and blessings of the Lord be yours, and may you know that the Lord of the Gospels can bless and empower us today.

Martyrs for the Kingdom

Matthew 2:13–18

"And when they [the wise men] were departed, behold, the angel of the Lord appeareth to Joseph in a dream, saying, Arise, and take the young child and his mother, and flee into Egypt, and be thou there until I bring thee word: for Herod will seek the young child to destroy him.

"When he arose, he took the young child and his mother by night, and departed into Egypt:

"And was there until the death of Herod: that it might be fulfilled which was spoken of the Lord by the prophet, saying, Out of Egypt have I called my son.

"Then Herod, when he saw that he was mocked of the wise men, was exceeding wroth, and sent forth, and slew all the children that were in Bethlehem, and in all the coasts thereof, from two years old and under, according to the time which he had diligently enquired of the wise men.

"Then was fulfilled that which was spoken by Jeremy the prophet, saying,

"In Rama was there a voice heard, lamentation, and weeping, and great mourning, Rachel weeping for her children, and would not be comforted, because they are not." (Matthew 2:13–18.)

Zacharias and John, His Son, Were Martyred

"When Herod's edict went forth to destroy the young children, John was about six months older than Jesus, and came under this hellish edict, and Zacharias caused his mother to take him into the mountains, where he was raised on locusts and wild honey. When his father refused to disclose his hiding place, and being the officiating high priest at the Temple that year, was slain by Herod's order, between the porch and the altar, as Jesus said. [Later,] John's head was taken to Herod, the son of this infant murderer, in a charger—notwithstanding there was never a greater prophet born of a woman than him!" (*Teachings of the Prophet Joseph Smith* [Salt Lake City: Deseret Book Co., 1976], p. 261.)

Baptism with the Holy Ghost and with Fire

Matthew 3:11, 13–17

"I indeed baptize you with water unto repentance: but he that cometh after me is mightier than I, whose shoes I am not worthy to bear: he shall baptize you with the Holy Ghost, and with fire: . . .

"Then cometh Jesus from Galilee to Jordan unto John, to be baptized of him.

"But John forbad him, saying, I have need to be baptized of thee, and comest thou to me?

"And Jesus answering said unto him, Suffer it to be so now: for thus it becometh us to fulfil all righteousness. Then he suffered him.

"And Jesus, when he was baptized, went up straightway out of the water: and, lo, the heavens were opened unto him, and he saw the Spirit of God descending like a dove, and lighting upon him:

"And lo a voice from heaven, saying, This is my beloved Son, in whom I am well pleased." (Matthew 3:11, 13–17.)

A Complete Baptism

President Lorenzo Snow described the experience he had after his baptism:

Some two or three weeks after I was baptized, one day while engaged in my studies, I began to reflect upon the fact that I had not obtained a knowledge of the truth of the work—that I had not realized the fulfilment of the promise "he that doeth my will shall know of the doctrine," and I began to feel very uneasy. I laid aside my books, left the house, and wandered around through the fields under the oppressive influence of a gloomy, disconsolate spirit, while an indescribable cloud of darkness seemed to envelop me. I had been accustomed, at the close of the day, to retire for secret prayer, to a grove a short distance from my lodgings, but at this time I felt no inclination to do so. The spirit of prayer had departed and the heavens seemed like brass over my head. At length, realizing that the usual time had come for secret prayer, I concluded I would not forego my evening service, and, as a matter of formality, knelt as I was in the habit of doing, and in my accustomed retired place, but not feeling as I was wont to feel.

I had no sooner opened my lips in an effort to pray, than I heard a sound, just above my head, like the rustling of silken robes, and immediately the Spirit of God descended upon me, completely enveloping my whole person, filling me, from the crown of my head to the soles of my feet, and O, the joy and happiness I felt! No language can describe the almost instantaneous transition from a dense cloud of mental and spiritual darkness into a refulgence of light and knowledge, as it was at that time imparted to my understanding. I then received a perfect knowledge that God lives, that Jesus Christ is the Son of God, and of the restoration of the holy priesthood and the fullness of the Gospel. It was a complete baptism—a tangible immersion in the heavenly principle or element, the Holy Ghost; and even more real and physical in its effects upon every part of my system than the immersion by water; dispelling forever, so long as reason and memory last, all possibility of doubt or fear in relation to the fact handed down to us historically, that the "Babe of Bethlehem" is truly the Son of God; also the fact that he is now being revealed to the children of men, and communicating knowledge, the same as in the apostolic times. I was perfectly satisfied, as well I might be, for my expectations were more than realized, I think I may safely say in an infinite degree.

I cannot tell how long I remained in the full flow of the blissful enjoyment and divine enlightenment, but it was several minutes before the celestial element which filled and surrounded me began gradually to withdraw. On arising from my kneeling posture, with my heart swelling with gratitude to God, beyond the power of expression, I felt—I knew that he had conferred on me what only an omnipotent being can confer—that which is of greater value than all the wealth and honors worlds can bestow. That night, as I retired to rest, the same wonderful manifestations were repeated, and continued to be for several successive nights. The sweet remembrance of those glorious experiences, from that time to the present, bring them fresh before me, imparting an inspiring influence which pervades my whole being and I trust will to the close of my earthly existence. (In William E. Berrett and Alma P. Burton, *Readings in LDS Church History* [Salt Lake City: Deseret Book Co., 1953], 1:89–90.)

"Get Thee Hence, Satan"

Matthew 4:1–11

Then was Jesus led up of the Spirit into the wilderness to be tempted of the devil.

And when he had fasted forty days and forty nights, he was afterward an hungred.

And when the tempter came to him, he said, If thou be the Son of God, command that these stones be made bread.

But he answered and said, It is written, Man shall not live by bread alone, but by every word that proceedeth out of the mouth of God.

Then the devil taketh him up into the holy city, and setteth him on a pinnacle of the temple,

And saith unto him, If thou be the Son of God, cast thyself down: for it is written, He shall give his angels charge concerning thee: and in their hands they shall bear thee up, lest at any time thou dash thy foot against a stone.

Jesus said unto him, It is written again, Thou shalt not tempt the Lord thy God.

Again, the devil taketh him up into an exceeding high mountain, and sheweth him all the kingdoms of the world, and the glory of them;

And saith unto him, All these things will I give thee, if thou wilt fall down and worship me.

Then saith Jesus unto him, Get thee hence, Satan: for it is written, Thou shalt worship the Lord thy God, and him only shalt thou serve.

Then the devil leaveth him, and, behold, angels came and ministered unto him. (Matthew 4:1–11.)

"Cease Tempting Me"

This experience was related by Elder Moses Thatcher, former member of the Quorum of the Twelve Apostles:

I heard a story in regard to a brother in Farmington a few years ago. The question of gathering the poor saints from England came up in an evening meeting.

The brother had two cows, and he donated one for the purpose mentioned. In going home a spirit of darkness said unto him: "You have been very foolish. You have given away one of the two cows you possessed, while Brother so-and-so, a much wealthier man than you, has only given five dollars."

"Now, you have done a wrong thing, a foolish thing." And thus was this brother tempted until he turned around and said, as though addressing himself to Satan: "If you don't cease tempting me, I will go back to the bishop, and give him the other one."

As the congregation broke into laughter, Elder Thatcher said, "Now, that is just as I feel. If at any time the Lord has blessed me with means, and I am tempted not to do as I should, because of the actions of others, I hope I shall always when tempted, feel to draw near unto the Lord, and ask His assistance." (As quoted in Jack E. Jarrard, "Vignettes of Faith," *Church News*, 15 January 1977, p. 16.)

"Blessed Are the Peacemakers"

Matthew 5:9

"Blessed are the peacemakers: for they shall be called the children of God" (Matthew 5:9).

"The Lord Was Going to Talk Now"

President J. Reuben Clark, Jr., once told the following story about President Brigham Young:

"To this point runs a simple story my father told me as a boy, I do not know on what authority, but it illustrates the point. His story was that during the excitement incident to the coming of Johnston's Army, Brother Brigham preached to the people in a morning meeting a sermon vibrant with defiance to the approaching army and declaring an intention to oppose and drive them back. In the afternoon meeting he arose and said that Brigham Young had been talking in the morning, but the Lord was going to talk now. He then delivered an address, the tempo of which was the opposite from the morning talk." (*Melchizedek Priesthood Study Guide* [Salt Lake City: The Church of Jesus Christ of Latter-day Saints, 1969–70], p. 222.)

Let Your Light Shine

Matthew 5:14–16

"Ye are the light of the world. A city that is set on an hill cannot be hid.

"Neither do men light a candle, and put it under a bushel, but on a candlestick; and it giveth light unto all that are in the house.

"Let your light so shine before men, that they may see your good works, and glorify your Father which is in heaven." (Matthew 5:14–16.)

The Parable of the Two Lamps

Elder James E. Talmage, a former member of the Council of the Twelve Apostles, as a student had a fine oil-burning study lamp, which he carefully trimmed daily and greatly used and enjoyed. He said that this "student lamp" was one of the best of its kind, purchased with his hard-earned savings. "It was counted among my most cherished possessions."

Elder Talmage related an experience he had concerning this highly efficient little lamp:

> One summer evening I sat musing studiously and withal restfully in the open air outside the door of the room in which I lodged and studied. A stranger approached. I noticed that he carried a satchel. He was affable and entertaining. I

brought another chair from within, and we chatted together till the twilight had deepened into dusk, the dusk into darkness.

Then he said: "You are a student, and doubtless have much work to do o'nights. What kind of lamp do you use?" And without waiting for a reply he continued: "I have a superior lamp I should like to show you, a lamp designed and constructed according to the latest achievements of applied science, far surpassing anything heretofore produced as a means of artificial lighting."

I replied with confidence . . . : "My friend, I have a lamp, one that has been tested and proved. It has been to me a companion through many a long night. . . . I have trimmed and cleaned it today; it is ready for the lighting. Step inside; I will show you my lamp, then you may tell me whether yours can possibly be better."

We entered my study room, and with a feeling which I assume is akin to that of the athlete about to enter a contest with one whom he regards as a pitiably inferior opponent, I put the match to my well-trimmed Argand.

My visitor was voluble in his praise. It was the best lamp of its kind he said. He averred that he had never seen a lamp in better trim. He turned the wick up and down and pronounced the adjustment perfect. . . .

"Now," said he, "with your permission I'll light my lamp." He took from his satchel a lamp then known as the "Rochester." It had a chimney which, compared with mine, was as a factory smoke-stack alongside a house flue. Its hollow wick was wide enough to admit my four fingers. Its light made bright the remotest corner of my room. In its brilliant blaze my own little Argand wick burned a weak, pale yellow. Until that moment of convincing demonstration I had never known the dim obscurity in which I had lived and labored, studied and struggled.

"I'll buy your lamp," said I; "you need neither explain nor argue further." I took my new acquisition to the laboratory that same night, and [found that it burned] fully four times the intensity of my student lamp.

Two days after purchasing, I met the lamp-peddler on the street, about noontime. To my inquiry he replied that business was good; the demand for his lamps was greater than the factory supply. "But," said I, "you are not working today?" His rejoinder was a lesson. "Do you think that I would be so foolish as to go around trying to sell lamps in the daytime? Would you have bought one if I had lighted it for you when the sun was shining? I chose the time to show the superiority of my lamp over yours; and you were eager to own the better one I offered, were you not?"

Such is the story. Now consider the application of a part, a very small part, thereof.

"Let your light so shine before men, that they may see your good works, and glorify your Father, which is in heaven."

The man who would sell me a lamp did not disparage mine. He placed his greater light alongside my feebler flame, and I hastened to obtain the better.

The missionary servants of the Church of Jesus Christ today are sent forth, not to assail or ridicule the beliefs of men, but to set before the world a superior light, by which the smoky dimness of the flickering flames of man-made creeds shall be apparent. The work of the Church is constructive, not destructive. (*The Parables of James E. Talmage*, comp. Albert L. Zobell, Jr. [Salt Lake City: Deseret Book Co., 1973], pp. 1–6.)

"Love Your Enemies"

Matthew 5:44, 10

"But I say unto you, Love your enemies, bless them that curse you, do good to them that hate you, and pray for them which despitefully use you, and persecute you."

"Blessed are they which are persecuted for righteousness' sake: for theirs is the kingdom of heaven." (Matthew 5:44, 10.)

Stuck in the Same Ditch

A saintly life invites one to pray for his enemies.

A wonderful Sunday School teacher once inspired my classmates and me, almost "stabbed" us all wide awake as would a divine surgeon, with the necessity of living daily in a manner pleasing to the Lord. He made us feel that our sacred scriptures could always be a point of reference that would lead us to God's celestial kingdom. A powerful testimony of this came to me as a result of an experience in my daily life, an experience that was truly a crossroads to me.

In my home town was a large pea factory. Peas were never picked in the patch; they were cut in the vine like hay, and loaded—green vines and all—on a hay wagon. A relatively small forkful could seem like a load of lead.

One morning as I was mowing some alfalfa, the fieldman from the factory came to me and said, "Your pea patch is ready right now to be harvested." This is a crucial point—a few hours of too much sunshine turns peas in a pod from first-class to hard tack. Much value of the crop is lost if it is not cut on time.

I moved my team and hay-cutting equipment to the five-acre pea patch and in a short time had cut all the hayrack would hold; in fact, it was all my small team could pull. With some effort and the help of a switch, I managed to get the team to pull the load to the hardened field road. Then we proceeded toward the factory a mile away. However, I had forgotten all about the old field ditch, full of water, which my team had to cross. Would I ever make it?

I soon discovered the answer. Approaching the ditch, I first gave the team a much-needed rest. Then, with positive urging, they shot across the ditch—but the front wheels hit the mud and sank up to the hub!

The only solution was for me to unload all the peas on the ground, pull the empty wagon across, and then proceed to carry the peas and replace them upon the wagon. The very thought made me tired. If only another team and wagon would appear on the scene—maybe two teams could pull me out!

Then up the road I could see an outfit coming in my direction. Help was in sight. As the wagon came closer, however, my heart sank. It was my neighbor who lived down the road and who did not help anyone. He didn't have to—he was rich in worldly goods.

As he pulled up beside me, he stopped his outfit and smilingly said, "So, you're stuck, are you, Lee?" I was surprised he knew my name. He had never talked to me before. I replied that my load was too big for my small team. His smile grew larger as he said, "Well, good luck to you," and away he went down the lane.

Never was I so angry! What I called him cannot be printed—I even spoke in Danish so my team couldn't understand! For the moment I reappraised the law of Moses. I looked up into the sky and said, "Oh, Father, give me the chance to meet him on the desert sometime, choking for a good drink of water. Let me have a barrel of water in my truck so I can pour it out onto the sand and tell him to scratch."

Somehow I managed to get to the factory. I succeeded in getting all of my peas harvested in time, and though my feelings were still on edge they had mellowed somewhat.

Evil seldom requires a down payment; it's like installment buying. My hope—and my day—finally arrived. A few days later, while proceeding to my farm, as I approached this road-block to my farming efforts, the ditch, I nearly choked with happiness. I found my unobliging neighbor stuck in the same ditch with a load of peas!

Before I reached the scene of trouble, like a bolt of light-ning my Sunday School teacher's lesson on retaliation came to my mind. I tried to unload the thought, but it was deeply entrenched in my soul. Our Savior said, "And whosoever shall compel thee to go a mile, go with him twain." (Matthew 5:41.) Now or never was my life to be molded by love or ha-tred. The Lord had said, "Agree with thine adversary quickly, whiles thou art in the way with him." (Matthew 5:25.) I did! I kicked the adversary off the wagon.

As I pulled up beside my brother, I stopped and repeated to him his own words: "So you're stuck, are you, brother?" I hoped he would learn from this new experience the lesson that Cain learned in the garden, that there is no such thing as liberty without law.

My neighbor responded that he could not proceed with-out help. I did not wait longer. I jumped off my wagon, took from it a long chain, and secured it properly onto the end of his wagon tongue. Then the two teams put their shoulders to the wheel and in short order they were all standing on dry ground.

In deep embarrassment, my neighbor said, "Thanks, Lee. I appreciate your kindness." Then he added, "How much do I owe you?"

My reply was not altogether honest. "I enjoyed helping you out of that ditch," I said.

We both went on our way rejoicing. I could hardly hold my team—they seemed to want to trot. And I caught myself whistling and singing "Come, Come Ye Saints."

A couple of days later I found a new bridge over the ditch. I smiled as I learned who had obliged all the north field farmers with this needed contribution.

Two weeks later, while cutting more hay one day, I no-ticed a man coming down through my field. It was my neigh-bor. "Let your team have a break, while we settle the problems of the world," he said. So we visited for a few minutes. Then, as he started to leave, he looked squarely at me and, in halting phrases, apologized for leaving me in the ditch.

I have often wondered just which one of us was the un-neighborly one. When had I ever volunteered to him any kindness? The injured one may well be the one at times who seeks confrontation and better understanding. We both learned a valuable lesson that day. (Leland E. Anderson, *Stories of Power and Purpose* [Salt Lake City: Bookcraft, 1974], pp. 6–9.)

"I Am Your Brother"

President George F. Richards, of the Council of the Twelve Apostles, spoke in general conference about loving one's enemies. His talk was given in October 1946, just one year after World War II ended.

If such love obtained in the world today as the Lord intended that it should, love of God and love of fellow men, there would be no wars, contentions, and strife among the children of men. And that there is such, is due to an indifference by men to heed the admonitions and teachings of our Lord and Savior Jesus Christ.

I profess love for you, my brethren, sisters, and friends, my hearers. I hope to be able to comply with the law to the extent that I can love all who hear my voice, whether they be in the Church or out of the Church, whether they be good or bad, whatever their condition of life. They are the children of our Eternal Father; they are our brothers and sisters. . . .

I have seldom mentioned this to other people, but I do not know why I should not. It seems to me appropriate in talking along this line. I dreamed that I and a group of my own associates found ourselves in a courtyard where, around the outer edge of it, were German soldiers—and Führer Adolph Hitler was there with his group, and they seemed to be sharpening their swords and cleaning their guns, and making preparations for a slaughter of some kind, or an execution.

We knew not what, but, evidently we were the objects. But presently a circle was formed and this Führer and his men were all within the circle, and my group and I were circled on the outside, and he was sitting on the inside of the circle with his back to the outside, and when we walked around and I got directly opposite to him, I stepped inside the circle and walked across to where he was sitting, and spoke to him in a manner something like this:

"I am your brother. You are my brother. In our heavenly home we lived together in love and peace. Why can we not so live here on the earth?"

And it seemed to me that I felt in myself, welling up in my soul, a love for that man, and I could feel that he was having the same experience, and presently he arose, and we embraced each other and kissed each other, a kiss of affection.

Then the scene changed so that our group was within the circle, and he and his group were on the outside, and when he came around to where I was standing, he stepped inside the circle and embraced me again, with a kiss of affection.

I think the Lord gave me that dream. Why should I dream of this man, one of the greatest enemies of mankind, and one of the wickedest, but that the Lord should teach me that I must love my enemies, and I must love the wicked as well as the good?

Now, who is there in this wide world that I could not love under those conditions, if I could only continue to feel as I felt then? I have tried to maintain this feeling and, thank the Lord, I have no enmity toward any person in this world; I can forgive all men, so far as I am concerned, and I am happy in doing so and in the love which I have for my fellow men. (In Conference Report, October 1946, pp. 138, 140.)

Perfection

Matthew 5:48

"Be ye therefore perfect, even as your Father which is in heaven is perfect" (Matthew 5:48).

God's Plan for Us

Change often involves pain, uncomfortable adjustment, and time. But the change that the gospel of Jesus Christ makes in our nature is for the better. Our Heavenly Father loves us too much to leave us as we are. He expects us to become something greater.

As C. S. Lewis indicated in a parable borrowed from George MacDonald, we cannot clearly see God's plan for us, but if we could it would be marvelous to behold: "Imagine yourself as a living house. God comes in to rebuild that house. At first, perhaps, you can understand what He is doing. He is getting the drains right and stopping the leaks in the roof and so on: you knew that those jobs needed doing and so you are not surprised. But presently he starts knocking the house about in a way that hurts abominably and does not seem to make sense. What on earth is He up to? The explanation is that He is building quite a different house from the one you thought of—throwing out a new wing here, putting on an extra floor there, running up towers, making courtyards. You thought you were going to be made into a decent little cottage: but He is building a palace." (C. S. Lewis, *Mere Christianity*, New York: MacMillan Publishing Co., 1960, p. 174.)

Sacrificial Service

Matthew 6:3–4

"But when thou doest alms, let not thy left hand know what thy right hand doeth:

"That thine alms may be in secret: and thy Father which seeth in secret himself shall reward thee openly" (Matthew 6: 3–4).

Gospel Givers

President A. Theodore Tuttle of the First Council of the Seventy taught seminary in Brigham City, Utah, for a time. While there he became acquainted with a bishop who owned many acres of land.

One year [the bishop] was blessed with an exceptionally large crop. He had sold thousands of bushels of hard wheat. When he went out to get the last load from the threshing, with his big truck carrying about ten tons, he wondered what he would do with it. He had a big bank account, all his silos were filled with wheat, and thousands of bushels had been sold. He thought a while, then said, "I know what I'll do—I'll give it to Brother John."

Brother John, who lived in this bishop's ward, had just been married. He and his wife had built a large chicken coop and were raising white leghorn chickens so they would have eggs to sell.

The bishop felt that nothing would be better than to give this young couple a boost in life. I'm not unmindful of the rich man in the New Testament who had a similar experience, except that his experience ended terribly. When he looked at his crops and all his barns loaded, he said to himself, "What will I do with all this increase? I know what I will do; I will tear my barns down and will build bigger ones. I will load them with the fruits of my labors." This man had forgotten to distinguish between what was the Lord's and what was his.

So the bishop drove up to the home of Brother John, backed his truck into the lot, and went up and knocked on the door. When he found there was no one home, he said, "Thank the Lord." Then he backed up against the big empty silo and put the machinery to work, and it wasn't long until he had the silo nearly filled with wheat. Then he drove off.

Two or three weeks passed. One day he met the young man on the sidewalk downtown. Brother John said to him, "Bishop, I have a problem. Someone by mistake has emptied a load of wheat and filled my silo. Now my chickens got into some of it this morning, and they sure like it, but I'm sure some farmer had a helper who didn't know where to unload it and put it in my granary by mistake. I'm wondering, inasmuch as you're a farmer, if you know anyone else who's been hauling grain into town."

With a twinkle in his eye, the bishop responded: "Brother John, if I were you, I would never try to find out who that man was."

Then Brother John realized the answer. He grabbed the bishop by the hand and said, "God bless you, dear bishop. I think I knew all the time who had done that work." The young man whipped out his checkbook, opened it, got out a pen, and started to write out a check. "How much do I owe you for that wheat?" he asked.

The bishop said, "John, put that checkbook back in your pocket. And as long as you live, don't think you owe me anything. If you live to be a million years old, you could not pay me for that wheat."

So both of them went on their way, rejoicing in the commandment of the Lord to love your neighbor as yourself.

A couple of weeks later was Thanksgiving, and the bishop went down to the meat locker to get some choice meat for Thanksgiving dinner. As he opened the door, he saw that the locker was filled with dressed chickens. He smiled, took what he needed, and went on his way with a lighter step.

A week later he met John on the street and said, "John, I have a problem. Someone by mistake has put a lot of dressed chickens in one of my meat lockers. And since you're in the chicken business, I thought you might know who's been killing chickens around town, because I want to pay for them."

John replied, "Bishop, if I were you I would never try to find out." At that, the bishop pulled out of his pocketbook a roll of bills and started to peel off some of the big ones. But John said, "You put that money back in your pocket. If you live to be a million years old, you couldn't pay me for those chickens."

This is the true spirit of the gospel of Jesus Christ. (Leland E. Anderson, *Stories of Power and Purpose* [Salt Lake City: Bookcraft, 1974], pp. 68–70.)

"Seek Ye First the Kingdom of God"

Matthew 6:24–33

No man can serve two masters: for either he will hate the one, and love the other; or else he will hold to the one, and despise the other. Ye cannot serve God and mammon.

Therefore I say unto you, Take no thought for your life, what ye shall eat, or what ye shall drink; nor yet for your body, what ye shall put on. Is not the life more than meat, and the body than raiment?

Behold the fowls of the air: for they sow not, neither do they reap, nor gather into barns; yet your heavenly Father feedeth them. Are ye not much better than they?

Which of you by taking thought can add one cubit unto his stature?

And why take ye thought for raiment? Consider the lilies of the field, how they grow; they toil not, neither do they spin:

And yet I say unto you, That even Solomon in all his glory was not arrayed like one of these.

Wherefore, if God so clothe the grass of the field, which to day is, and to morrow is cast into the oven, shall he not much more clothe you, O ye of little faith?

Therefore take no thought, saying, What shall we eat? or, What shall we drink? or, Wherewithal shall we be clothed?

(For after all these things do the Gentiles seek:) for your heavenly Father knoweth that ye have need of all these things.

But seek ye first the kingdom of God, and his righteousness; and all these things shall be added unto you. (Matthew
6:24–33.)

"Your Children Shall Never Beg for Bread"

John Tanner was born August 15, 1778, in Rhode Island.
When he was thirteen, his family moved to New York. John became a farmer, like his father, and in 1800 he married Tabitha
Bentley. Just a year later, Tabitha passed away, two weeks after the
birth of their first child. John later married Lydia Stuart, and together they had nine sons and three daughters. But Lydia died in
1825, leaving John with a large family to care for. He later married a third wife, Elizabeth Besswick, and they had six sons and
two daughters. Notwithstanding the responsibilities associated
with such a large family, John worked hard and acquired large
tracts of land. His influence in the community was extensive, and
he was known for his benevolence, honesty, and integrity.

In 1832, John was crippled by a diseased leg. For six months
he was unable to walk or use his leg. He had a unique chair constructed that enabled him to move from place to place without
assistance. In September of that same year, notice was given that
two Mormon missionaries would be preaching at a place near
John Tanner's home. John attended the meeting and met Simeon
and Jared Carter. He first went to the meeting with the intention
of using the Bible to expose the fallacies of Mormonism. But long
before the meeting ended, John was genuinely touched. He invited the elders to his home where they could continue a conversation. By eleven o'clock that night, John wanted to be baptized,
but told the elders he couldn't "on account of my lameness."

As they discussed the ability of the Savior to heal all manner
of diseases, they asked Mr. Tanner if he thought that the gospel
had that same power in all ages. John answered that he did believe the Lord could heal him. Elder Jared Carter then commanded John Tanner in the name of Christ to walk. "I arose,
threw down my crutches, walked the floor back and forth, praised

God, and felt as light as a feather," John later said. That night he walked three-fourths of a mile to Lake George, where he was baptized by Simeon Carter. (See Maurice Tanner, comp., *Descendants of John Tanner* [The Tanner Family Association, 1942], pp. 14–15.)

When the call came to gather to Kirtland, John sold his businesses, property, and a hotel he owned to join with the Saints in Ohio.

> About the middle of December [John] received an impression by dream or vision of the night, that he was needed and must go immediately to the Church in the West. He told his family of the instruction he had received and forthwith made preparations for the start, while his neighbors, with deep regret at what they considered an insane purpose, tried their utmost to dissuade him; but he knew the will of God in the present crisis and nothing could deter him from doing it.
>
> On Christmas day he commenced his journey with all his earthly effects, and in the dead of Winter traveled the distance of five hundred miles, to Kirtland where he arrived about the 20th of January, 1835, on the Sabbath.
>
> On his arrival in Kirtland, he learned that at the time he received the impression that he must move immediately to the Church, the Prophet Joseph and some of the brethren had met in prayer-meeting and asked the Lord to send them a brother or some brethren with means to assist them to lift the mortgage on the farm upon which the temple was being built.
>
> The day after his arrival in Kirtland, by invitation from the prophet, he and his son, Sidney, met with the High Council, and were informed that the mortgage of the before mentioned farm was about to be foreclosed. Whereupon he loaned the prophet two thousand dollars and took his note on interest, with which amount the farm was redeemed. [John Tanner, "Sketch of an Elder's Life," in *Scraps of Biography* (Salt Lake City, 1883), 12.]

It is estimated that at various times John gave or loaned over fifty thousand dollars to Joseph Smith and the Church. By the time he was forced to leave Ohio with the Saints, he had lost a virtual fortune. . . .

Later John forgave the remaining debts incurred in Kirtland, as the following incident illustrates:

> At the April Conference in 1844, [John] was called on a mission to the Eastern States. Before starting, he went to Nauvoo, where he saw the Prophet Joseph, and, meeting him on the street, gave him his note of hand for the two thousand dollars loaned in Kirtland, January 1835, to redeem the temple land. The Prophet asked him what he wanted done with the note. Elder Tanner replied, "Brother Joseph, you are welcome to it." The Prophet then laid his right hand heavily on Elder Tanner's shoulder, saying, "God bless you, Father Tanner; your children shall never beg bread." [Ibid., 16.] (Karl Ricks Anderson, *Joseph Smith's Kirtland* [Deseret Book Co., Salt Lake City, 1989], pp. 16–17.)

John Tanner sacrificed everything he had for the gospel, and the promise given to him by the Prophet Joseph Smith has been literally fulfilled.

"I Never Knew You"

Matthew 7:21-23

"Not every one that saith unto me, Lord, Lord, shall enter into the kingdom of heaven; but he that doeth the will of my Father which is in heaven.

"Many will say to me in that day, Lord, Lord, have we not prophesied in thy name? and in thy name have cast out devils? and in thy name done many wonderful works?

"And then will I profess unto them, I never knew you: depart from me, ye that work iniquity." (Matthew 7:21-23.)

A Two-Year-Old Boy Who Knew the Savior

One sunny Arizona afternoon, my two-year-old son and I drove to the visitors' center at the Arizona Temple. I took Josh's hand as we approached the large double doors, hoping that even though he was so young, I would be able to teach him something about our Savior.

As I opened the door, the statue of Christ stood before us—with arms outstretched as if to beckon us. "Jesus!" Josh exclaimed, as if he were greeting a long-lost friend. Before I could stop him, Josh broke away from me and ran with open arms toward the statue. Darting under the rope barrier that surrounded the figure, he embraced the Savior's leg.

The guide, smiling, kindly asked Josh to step outside the rope barrier. He spoke with Josh briefly about our visit there, and then went on to welcome others who had come through the door.

I took Josh's hand, knelt beside him, and talked with him about Christ. Pointing out the nail wounds in the hands and feet of the statue, I told my son about the crucifixion.

Josh's little chin began to quiver as tears puddled in his eyes. "Who would do that to Jesus?" he whispered, not wanting to believe that anyone would do something so dreadful to someone he loved so much.

Our visit was short, yet Josh talked about it for many days afterward. He could not understand why anyone would want to hurt Jesus, his friend. And I learned from that visit, too. I found out that while I may know *about* Jesus, it was my sweet two-year-old son who *knew* the Savior. (Sandi Leavitt, "And a Little Child Shall Lead Them," *Ensign*, February 1986, p. 53; italics in original.)

"Master,
the Tempest Is Raging!"

Matthew 8:23–27

"And when he was entered into a ship, his disciples followed him.

"And, behold, there arose a great tempest in the sea, insomuch that the ship was covered with the waves: but he was asleep.

"And his disciples came to him, and awoke him, saying, Lord, save us: we perish.

"And he saith unto them, Why are ye fearful, O ye of little faith? Then he arose, and rebuked the winds and the sea; and there was a great calm.

"But the men marvelled, saying, What manner of man is this, that even the winds and the sea obey him!" (Matthew 8:23–27.)

Prayer Calms the Sea

Many times the prayers of the Brethren and the members of the Church have been literally answered so that planned meetings and sacred occasions would not have to be dispensed with because of stormy weather.

On Sunday, 9 January 1955, President David O. McKay was speaking to the Saints on the Island of Suva, in the South Pacific.

He pointed out that the meeting being held that day was very significant and of historical importance. There had been no intention of remaining in Suva over Sunday because the planned schedule of travel called for the McKay party to be somewhere between Suva and Tonga, but because of hurricane warnings, they were delayed a whole day. They were not aware that there were members of the Church in Suva. President McKay pointed out that thirty-four years ago Elder Hugh J. Cannon and he had stopped at Suva on the SS *Tofua*, but had decided that the time was not ripe for the preaching of the gospel to the people of Fiji. But on this day, . . . because of a change in their schedule which came about by reason of the hurricane warnings, they were here to preach the gospel in Suva, and to commence the building up of the kingdom of God. President McKay then said: *"Surely God has had a hand in changing our schedule so that we can be with you, the members of the Church here on this island."* He told them that the eyes of the people of the island would be upon them, and that they must have good thoughts and render good deeds. He said that every member should be a missionary and urged all to work together for the acquiring of land upon which to build a chapel. He promised that if they would be faithful, they would have peace of mind, that their faith would be increased, and their testimonies strengthened. He blessed them that peace might be in their hearts and in their homes with their families, and urged them all to work unitedly for the spreading of the gospel.

Following the meeting a dinner of native dishes was served to all the members. As they were gathered around the table, it was brought to their attention that one of the boys and a girl (now a grown man, and a woman) had been on the ship with President McKay and Elder Hugh J. Cannon thirty-four years ago traveling from Tonga to Hapaai where they had encountered a very severe storm. They described how high the waves were and how rough the sea, and that they had appealed to Apostle McKay, and he offered a word of prayer, following which not only the waves had subsided, but also the sea had become calm. (Clare Middlemiss, *Cherished Experiences* [Salt Lake City: Deseret Book Co., 1955], pp. 51–52, emphasis in original.)

"Where Is Your Faith?"

On many occasions the elements have been tempered in order that assignments might be carried out and destinations reached.

In Bern, Switzerland, in 1953, it had been raining six weeks prior to the date of the dedication of the temple site. After prayer and fasting by the missionaries and Saints, on the day of the dedication, Wednesday, August 5, 1953, the sun came out; the clouds disappeared, and there was a beautiful day for the open-air meeting. However, that night it started to rain again, and it rained all day the following day. "Surely," said President McKay, "the prayers for good weather during the dedicatory services were answered." In London there was a similar experience. When it came time to dedicate the London Temple site, although it had rained steadily previous to the date of the dedication, bright, clear weather prevailed throughout the dedicatory services held on August 10, 1953.

Following his 35,000-mile journey in 1954 to the British Isles, Switzerland, South Africa, South America, Central America, and Mexico, President McKay expressed gratitude for their safe return from their travels, during which they had encountered electrical storms in mid-air, and other incidents wherein they felt divine intervention in their behalf.

Elder Franklin J. Murdock in his day-by-day journal of President and Mrs. McKay's 45,000-mile-journey by air to Australia, New Zealand, and the Islands of the South Pacific said: "How fortunate we have been all along the way! It just seems that a protecting hand has gone ahead and directed the hurricanes in another direction as we needed to land, and even though we are in the rainy season, the weather for all occasions has been clear and warm, and not one meeting has had to be changed or broken up because of inclement weather. Good weather has been where we needed it to carry out the assignments, and the members have marveled at the sudden changes in the weather as each meeting or assignment has started. Surely the Lord is with us and has blessed us with good health, good spirits, and good protection! (January 15, 1955.)

"On January 15, 1955, the day of the dedication of the Church edifice at Sauniatu, Samoa, and the open-air services held at the David 0. McKay Monument, although it had been raining previously, we encountered beautiful weather. As we bade farewell to the happy faces at Sauniatu, and took a last glance at the monument, the rains started; but the meetings were completed, and we were safely in the automobile ready to drive back to Apia."

Elder Howard B. Stone, president of the Samoan Mission, reported the following concerning President and Mrs. McKay's visit to Samoa:

"The night before we landed at Aitutaki in the Cook Island group, January 18, 1955, Elders Bushoff and Johnson, with sixty-six Saints and eighty-five nonmembers had traveled a distance of ten miles in three whaleboats and had slept under the stars and palm trees so that they could meet with President McKay and his party the next day for one short hour while the seaplane was refueling prior to its departure for Tahiti. We held a meeting in the grove of palm trees on that little island, after which all of the natives, who incidentally, were very shy, quietly walked by in single file to shake hands with the Prophet of God and other members of the party. We were threatened with rain for the second time in a week, but in each instance, after a prayer in our hearts, a rainbow appeared in the horizon, and the rainstorm passed over us. The weather has been perfect during the entire trip, even though there have been hurricanes and tropical squalls on all sides of us."

On Saturday, February 10, 1955, ground-breaking ceremonies were held for the Church college of Hawaii at Laie where the junior college will be built. All the Saints and missionaries had fasted and prayed that they would have good weather for this important occasion. Brother Murdock in his report said: "There was a steady downpour of rain as we drove up to the property where the new Church junior college is to be built. I looked out from the car window, and said: 'President McKay, you're not going out in this downpour, are you?' President McKay answered unhesitatingly, 'Come on; where is your faith?' Then he opened the car door and stepped out. As he did so, the rains ceased and the sun came out. It is truly remarkable how the weather cooperates with us."

On January 31, 1955, just before President McKay and his traveling companions left Sydney, Australia, by plane for Brisbane, Australia, one of the missionaries, a member of the party, offered a prayer at the airport asking for God's protection on their journey.

How well that prayer was answered is indicated in the following report by Elder Murdock:

"The trip from Sydney to Brisbane was made in a DC-4. The journey was smooth and without incident until we had been going for about an hour and a half. We were traveling at about 250 miles an hour. President Waters, a counselor in the mission presidency, had gone up into the cockpit with the pilot who had agreed to circle over Brisbane in order that we could get a look at the city lighted up at night.

"Suddenly the pilot noticed a heavy rain and lightning storm in our pathway and seemed greatly concerned as to what the consequences might be. As the plane neared the storm area, the lights in the plane suddenly went out and then on, and the storm had disappeared. The pilot could not understand what had happened nor where the storm had gone, but it had vanished, and the plane went on its course without further incident."

Thus this world-wide missionary, our President, who constantly seeks the Lord with all his soul, who is deeply conscious of his dependence upon him for guidance and assistance, has had and is still having the protecting care of our Heavenly Father throughout all his travels. (Clare Middlemiss, *Cherished Experiences* [Salt Lake City: Deseret Book Co., 1955], pp. 44–48.)

Storm on All Sides of the Grove

I was very small when we lived in Nauvoo, but I always attended the meetings. The most striking thing I remember was a prophecy Joseph Smith made, which I saw fulfilled immediately. I was at the funeral service of King Follett, in the Nauvoo Grove. A heavy thunderstorm arose. The people became frightened and started to go home. But the Prophet arose and told the multitude that if they would remain still and pray in their hearts the storm would not molest them in their services.

They did as they were bidden, and the storm divided over the grove. I well remember how it was storming on all sides of the grove, yet it was calm around us as if there was no sign of a storm so near by.

I thought as I sat there that the Lord was speaking through Joseph. (Mary C. Westover, as quoted in *They Knew the Prophet*, comps. Hyrum L. Andrus and Helen Mae Andrus [Salt Lake City: Bookcraft, 1974], p. 167.)

Crossing the Channel in Safety

(Early in 1896, the First Presidency of the Church called Edward Wood to return to Samoa as mission president. Prior to his departure he was given a missionary blessing by Seymour B. Young in which President Wood was promised that "the elements will be subject to your control. They shall neither destroy you nor retard your travel on land or sea." For one who knew the dangers of traveling about the Samoan Mission, this blessing must have been of great comfort to him then, and even more so on April 7, 1896, when President Wood recorded:)

"We had a mission conference appointed at our headquarters. I was visiting on Savaii, our largest island, and with a number of natives planned to leave this island and cross the channel between the two islands, about fifteen miles distant. While we were holding a meeting, a strong wind arose, making a very rough sea covered with whitecaps and very heavy swells, and making it extremely dangerous for small boats such as we had for the crossing. What a disappointment it would be for those at the conference if we did not arrive at the meeting."

(It was then that one of the natives suggested that the group repair to the sandy beach to hold an open-air prayer service. The native then requested that President Wood offer a prayer and rebuke the wind and waves so that they could cross the channel in safety. The group then sang a hymn of praise to the Lord and knelt on the beach as President Wood asked the Lord to calm enough of the surface of the ocean so that their boats might cross over the channel in safety.)

"After that prayer," Elder Wood continued, "we bade goodbye to those who were remaining on the island and launched our boats and were soon out of the lagoon in mid-ocean. To our great surprise and gratitude, a smooth lane lay before us all the way across. It was about one hundred feet wide, while on either side the waves were mountainous and the wind very strong. As soon as we set foot on the beach of the other island, we again knelt in prayer and thanked God for preserving our lives and for calming the ocean.

"During the conference most of the native Saints in our company bore testimony to our deliverance through the goodness of God in calming the waves for our crossing. Surely it was a time of general rejoicing, for the promise given two years earlier in a missionary blessing had been marvelously fulfilled." (As quoted in Margie Calhoun Jensen, comp., *Stories of Insight and Inspiration* [Salt Lake City: Bookcraft, 1976], pp. 30–31.)

Seeking After a Sign

Matthew 12:38–39

"Then certain of the scribes and of the Pharisees answered, saying, Master, we would see a sign from thee.

"But he answered and said unto them, An evil and adulterous generation seeketh after a sign; and there shall no sign be given to it." (Matthew 12:38–39.)

Signs Follow Believers

In the year 1841, three Elders—James M. Adams, James M. Emmett and Hiram Page—were traveling in Erie County, Pennsylvania, preaching the gospel. The opposing power, which is always ready to contest the ground with the Elders, inch by inch, manifested itself there in a most violent manner. As usual, this opposition came from those who professed to be Christians. . . .

The Elders were finally challenged to debate with a number of preachers, on the subject of the gospel. The challenge was accepted on condition that the preachers would confine their arguments to Bible proofs, which they agreed to do.

The discussion accordingly opened by Elder Adams preaching a discourse on the first principles of the gospel. He spoke in such a plain, pointed and forcible manner, that the opponents to the truth were disconcerted. When their turn to speak arrived, they laid aside the volume of inspiration which they had agreed to take as their guide, and commenced reading from Howe's "Mormonism Unveiled," a book written by one D.P. Hurlbut. This book contained the most glaring falsehoods and inconsistent ideas that wicked men could invent.

The umpires informed the preachers that they must not deviate from their written contract, but confine themselves to Bible proofs, as they had agreed to do. If the "Mormon" doctrine was false, it must be proved so from the Bible.

After the old preachers had tried in vain to produce any scripture proofs, or logic either, to sustain their false views, and the powerless form of religion which they held to, they were reinforced by a young Free-will Baptist preacher, named Solon Hill. It was soon evident that he could offer nothing in the way of argument. . . . Finally, however, he hit upon a plan which he seemed to think would enable him to come off victor.

Turning to Elder Adams, he said, "If you are a servant of God, as you boldly say you are, I demand a sign of you, to convince me that you are genuine."

Elder Adams told him that he had taken a dangerous stand; that signs followed believers, but did not go before them; that signs came by faith, not faith by signs. He informed him who the first sign-seeker was—Satan, whose children had always been faithful in following his example. He testified that the truths of heaven had been plainly laid before them, that the Spirit had given unmistakable evidence of its truth, and that unless he repented of his sins, rendered obedience to the gospel and lived up to its requirements, the curse of God would rest upon him.

The meeting was dismissed without the preachers being able to disprove any of the truths advanced by the Elders; the people were left to reflect at leisure upon what they had listened to, and the preacher, Hill, to accept the consequences of disobeying the servant of God.

After a lapse of sixteen years from the time of the events just narrated, I happened to be in the same part of Pennsylvania upon a mission.

Calling one day at a house to water my horse, I saw one of the most deformed and repulsive looking beings I ever beheld.

On arriving at my destination, I informed my brethren of the hideous sight I had met with, when I was told that the being I had seen was what was left of the man who had demanded a sign from a servant of God.

In 1878, Elder Butler, of Ogden, was on a mission to the same place, and I wrote to him for information concerning Hill. His reply was, "He is still alive, and an object of charity." (J.H. Van Natta, "Sign-Seeking," in *Four Faith Promoting Classics* [Salt Lake City: Bookcraft, 1968], pp. 53–54.)

Feeding a Multitude

Matthew 14:15–21

"And when it was evening, his disciples came to him, saying, This is a desert place, and the time is now past; send the multitude away, that they may go into the villages, and buy themselves victuals.

"But Jesus said unto them, They need not depart; give ye them to eat.

"And they say unto him, We have here but five loaves, and two fishes.

"He said, Bring them hither to me.

"And he commanded the multitude to sit down on the grass, and took the five loaves, and the two fishes, and looking up to heaven, he blessed, and brake, and gave the loaves to his disciples, and the disciples to the multitude.

"And they did all eat, and were filled: and they took up of the fragments that remained twelve baskets full.

"And they that had eaten were about five thousand men, beside women and children." (Matthew 14:15–21.)

Feeding the Five Hundred

Just feeding the five in my family sometimes feels overwhelming, so reading in the New Testament about Christ's miraculous feeding of the five thousand has always impressed me.

But I was also impressed one day as a good neighbor and Relief Society sister brought my family dinner after the birth of my third child. For more than twenty-five years, my neighbor has been taking dinners to families who need a helping hand. She has provided food on scores of occasions and must surely have fed several hundreds of hungry husbands and children. Although she has not miraculously fed five thousand people on an isolated hillside, she had worked her own quiet miracle in feeding the five hundred. Unknown numbers of casseroles, cakes, and salads have gone to nourish people just as dear to the Lord as those gathered on that ancient hillside.

I often wonder how many quiet "miracles" similar to hers are being worked by sisters with charity in their hearts and how much more I can learn to offer. (Diane L. Mangum, "Feeding the Five Hundred," *Ensign*, July 1984, p. 61.)

Mother Fed Five Thousand

There were mornings in mother's life when she got out of bed with an uncanny desire to "cook for an army." In our early years we children groaned at the prospect of helping her make huge mounds of potato or fruit salad and pans of meatloaf, enchiladas, or Swedish meatballs.

Such large quantities of food dulled our appetites for even our favorite dishes.

Mother never could explain the "why" behind her prompting, but those hectic days often ended with welcome, unexpected visits from traveling relatives, friends, and friends of friends who enjoyed all she had prepared. We children came to know that the still small voice can speak in very practical terms, and that with a trusting response, a modern-day "five thousand" could be fed.

However, one Saturday of special preparations passed into Sunday without a visitor. Then, after sacrament meeting, the phone rang and a neighbor's voice said, "Beth, some friends sent a family to stay with us while they go to the temple to be sealed. We haven't room. Have you?"

That was all mom needed. Five minutes later, as ten

strangers pulled into our driveway, we children were setting the table for yet another late Sunday supper.

This time was different, though. In the hustle and bustle mom spotted one small pair of eyes that seemed to need attention. Her welcoming words to the family were, "Let's get that boy to a doctor."

Dad called a good friend—an eye specialist—who identified a burrowing spore that, he said, would have caused permanent blindness if it had been left untreated any longer.

How thankful we were that even in the midst of confusion mother had heard and heeded the still small voice.

Later that night after the family was bedded down, mother discovered her next challenge. Laundering our guests' clothes in preparation for the important day ahead, she found that most of the shirts and blouses had not been strong enough to survive one last washing.

Then came a frantic inventory of our closets, late-night calls to neighbors, and an early-morning collection of beautiful, donated clothes. I'll always remember the pride in mother's eyes as she sent those parents and their eight children to the temple to be sealed "never looking better."

We learned later that they had saved money for their temple trip by living in the back of a large truck.

That family retained a special membership in mom's "five thousand," as did one of our neighbors, Ern, who lived in a one-room shack. For years his life was a mystery to us, although we knew that he had long been inactive in the Church. Perhaps his inactivity was due partially to his hunched back—the result of a poorly repaired bone fracture—or perhaps it was due to his lack of teeth, or his Word of Wisdom problems. Mom, though, prompted by that still, small voice, helped bring about a major change in his life.

For a long time, Ern declined our dinner invitations. Then mom, aware of his sensitivity over his lack of teeth, started sending Sunday dinner to his home where he could eat comfortably and privately.

But that was not his real "feeding." That came later in the week when he returned the dishes. Then, with an invitation to visit, he would spend most of a leisurely afternoon talking while mom worked and the younger children played around him. Other relationships developed, and in two years Ern cheerfully exchanged his usual seat on a bench in front of the courthouse for a seat in the temple, doing endowment work. But he always reserved one afternoon each week to return his dishes and visit with mom in the kitchen.

Such experiences over the years proved to us that mom's desire to "cook for any army" was really the work of an inspired and generous heart. Ern described her as "a mighty fine woman." She had the capacity to see that people not only needed food for their bodies, but food for their spirits, too. (Karen Christensen Luthy, "Mother Fed Five Thousand," *Ensign*, August 1978, pp. 64–66.)

Walking on the Sea

Matthew 14:22–33; John 6:19, 21

The Savior

"And straightway Jesus constrained his disciples to get into a ship, and to go before him unto the other side, while he sent the multitudes away.

"And when he had sent the multitudes away, he went up into a mountain apart to pray: and when the evening was come, he was there alone.

"But the ship was now in the midst of the sea, tossed with waves: for the wind was contrary.

"And in the fourth watch of the night Jesus went unto them, walking on the sea." (Matthew 14:22–25.)

"So when they had rowed about five and twenty or thirty furlongs, they see Jesus walking on the sea, and drawing nigh unto the ship: and they were afraid" (John 6:19).

"And when the disciples saw him walking on the sea, they were troubled, saying, It is a spirit; and they cried out for fear.

"But straightway Jesus spake unto them, saying, Be of good cheer; it is I; be not afraid." (Matthew 14:26–27.)

"Then they willingly received him into the ship" (John 6:21).

The Apostle Peter

"And Peter answered him and said, Lord, if it be thou, bid me come unto thee on the water.

"And he said, Come. And when Peter was come down out of the ship, he walked on the water, to go to Jesus.

"But when he saw the wind boisterous, he was afraid; and beginning to sink, he cried, saying, Lord, save me.

"And immediately Jesus stretched forth his hand, and caught him, and said unto him, O thou of little faith, wherefore didst thou doubt?

"And when they were come into the ship, the wind ceased.

"Then they that were in the ship came and worshipped him, saying, Of a truth thou art the Son of God." (Matthew 14:28–33.)

Joseph's Dream

In June, 1844, when Joseph Smith went to Carthage and delivered himself up to [Governor] Ford, I accompanied him, and while on the way thither, he related to me and his brother Hyrum the following dream:

He said: "While I was at Jordan's in Iowa the other night, I dreamed that myself and my brother Hyrum went on board of a large steamboat, lying in a small bay, near the great ocean. Shortly after we went on board there was an 'alarm of fire,' and I discovered that the boat had been anchored some distance from the shore, out in the bay, and that an escape from the fire, in the confusion, appeared hazardous; but, as delay was folly, I and Hyrum jumped overboard, and tried our faith at walking upon the water.

"At first we sank in the water nearly to our knees, but as we proceeded we increased in faith, and were soon able to walk upon the water. On looking towards the burning boat in the east, we saw that it was drifting towards the wharf and the town, with a great flame and clouds of smoke; and, as if by whirlwind, the town was taking fire, too, so that the scene of destruction and horror of the frightened inhabitants was terrible.

"We proceeded on the bosom of the mighty deep and were soon out of sight of land. The ocean was still; the rays of the sun were bright, and we forgot all the troubles of our Mother Earth. Just at that moment I heard the sound of a human voice, and, turning round, saw my brother Samuel H. approaching towards us from the east. We stopped and he came up. After a moment's conversation he informed me that he had been lonesome back, and had made up his mind to go with me across the mighty deep.

"We all started again, and in a short time were blest with the first sight of a city, whose gold and silver steeples and towers were more beautiful than any I had ever seen or heard of on earth. It stood, as it were, upon the western shore of the mighty deep we were walking on, and its order and glory seemed far beyond the wisdom of man. While we were gazing upon the perfection of the city, a small boat launched off from the port, and, almost as quick as thought, came to us. In an instant they took us on board and saluted us with a welcome, and with music such as is not on earth. The next scene, on landing, was more than I can describe: the greeting of old friends, the music from a thousand towers, and the light of God himself at the return of three of his sons, soothed my soul into a quiet and a joy that I felt as if I was truly in heaven. I gazed upon the splendor; I greeted my friends. I awoke, and lo, it was a dream!

"While I meditated upon such a marvelous scene, I fell asleep again, and behold I stood near the shore of the burning boat, and there was a great consternation among the officers, crew and passengers of the flaming craft, as there seemed to be much ammunition or powder on board. The alarm was given that the fire was near the magazine, and in a moment, suddenly, it blew up with a great noise, and sank in deep water with all on board. I then turned to the country east, among the bushy openings, saw William and Wilson Law endeavoring to escape from the wild beasts of the forest, but two lions rushed out of a thicket and devoured them. I awoke again."

I will say that Joseph never told this dream again, as he was martyred about two days after. I relate from recollection as nearly as I can. (*Almanac for the Year 1863* [Salt Lake City: Deseret News, 1862], pp. 27–28.)

"And He Healed Them"

Matthew 15:29–31; 21:14; Acts 3:1–10

"And Jesus departed from thence, and came nigh unto the sea of Galilee; and went up into a mountain, and sat down there.

"And great multitudes came unto him, having with them those that were lame, blind, dumb, maimed, and many others, and cast them down at Jesus' feet; and he healed them:

"Insomuch that the multitude wondered, when they saw the dumb to speak, the maimed to be whole, the lame to walk, and the blind to see: and they glorified the God of Israel." (Matthew 15:29–31.)

"And the blind and the lame came to him in the temple; and he healed them" (Matthew 21:14).

Peter and John Heal a Man Lame from Birth

Now Peter and John went up together into the temple at the hour of prayer, being the ninth hour.

And a certain man lame from his mother's womb was carried, whom they laid daily at the gate of the temple which is called Beautiful, to ask alms of them that entered into the temple;

Who seeing Peter and John about to go into the temple asked an alms.

And Peter, fastening his eyes upon him with John, said, Look on us.

And he gave heed unto them, expecting to receive something of them.

Then Peter said, Silver and gold have I none; but such as I have give I thee: In the name of Jesus Christ of Nazareth rise up and walk.

And he took him by the right hand, and lifted him up: and immediately his feet and ankle bones received strength.

And he leaping up stood, and walked, and entered with them into the temple, walking, and leaping, and praising God.

And all the people saw him walking and praising God:

And they knew that it was he which sat for alms at the Beautiful gate of the temple: and they were filled with wonder and amazement at that which had happened unto him. (Acts 3:1–10.)

"I Will Walk"

President Harold B. Lee said:

In Brazil . . . two of the elders came to me and said, "We have a family here that is investigating. They have a little boy who is six years old who has never walked. When we told him that there was going to be an apostle here tonight for the conference, the little boy said, "When the apostle comes, he will bless me and I will walk. . . ."

The elder said, "Would you be kind enough to join with us in blessing this little boy?" I replied that I would.

The president was busy with some other things at the conference, so I went with the two elders and the father carried this little boy in his arms and carried him in and sat him on a chair. The mother and two smaller children sat there, and the only impression I had as the elders and I put our hands on his head was that the little fellow sat there and cried all the time we were blessing him. He was overcome by something.

On my way home I got a letter from President Moyle who said, "We are anxious to have you come home and tell us about the healing that came to that little boy down in Brazil."

I hadn't heard anything about the outcome of the blessing, but when I arrived home I was shown a picture showing this little boy standing on his feet for the first time.

That miracle didn't come because of me; it didn't come because of the elders; this was because the Lord himself, by my hand and the hands of the elders, put his hands upon the head of that little boy by our hands and he received the strength . . . to stand on his feet for the first time since his birth. ("Speaking for Himself—President Lee's Stories," *Ensign*, February 1974, pp. 19–20.)

Great Multitudes
Made Whole

Matthew 15:30–31

"And great multitudes came unto him, having with them those that were lame, blind, dumb, maimed, and many others, and cast them down at Jesus' feet; and he healed them:

"Insomuch that the multitude wondered, when they saw the dumb to speak, the maimed to be whole, the lame to walk, and the blind to see: and they glorified the God of Israel." (Matthew 15:30–31.)

"See What You Have Done for Me"

Elder Matthew Cowley told the following experience:

I was down on the Indian reservation when I met a sister who had just joined the Church, a beautiful Navajo woman. My they dress beautifully down there. . . . Beautiful velvet dresses. . . . They get on these beautiful dresses and go out and buy their groceries at the trading post. Anyway, after I'd met this sister one of the missionaries called me off to the side and said, "A few months ago my companion and I went into a hogan and that lady, that Indian sister, was lying on the ground on a sheepskin. She had been lying there for six long years. We called on her, and when we were leaving she called us back and said in broken English, 'Isn't there something you do for sick people?' And we said, 'Yes.'

"She said, 'Please do it for me.' " So they got down on their knees and administered to her, by the authority of the priesthood and in the name of Jesus Christ. Then they left, and they weren't away fifty yards when she came out of the hogan after them and said, "Come back and see what you have done for me." She walked. God does have control of all of these elements. You and I can reach out, and if it's His will we can bring those elements under our control for His purposes. ("Miracles," in *Speeches of the Year: 1953–54* [Provo: Brigham Young University, 1953], p. 10.)

"She Threw Off Her Bandages"

Parley P. Pratt wrote:

In the morning I commenced a regular visit to each of the clergy of the place, introducing myself and my errand. I was absolutely refused hospitality, and denied the opportunity of preaching in any of their houses or congregations. Rather an unpromising beginning, thought I, considering the prophecies on my head concerning Toronto. However, nothing daunted, I applied to the Sheriff for the use of the Court House, and then to the authorities for a public room in the market place; but with no better success. What could I do more? I had exhausted my influence and power without effect. I now repaired to a pine grove just out of the town, and, kneeling down, called on the Lord, bearing testimony of my unsuccessful exertions; my inability to open the way; at the same time asking Him in the name of Jesus to open an effectual door for His servant to fulfill his mission in that place.

I then arose and again entered the town, and going to the house of John Taylor, had placed my hand on my baggage to depart from a place where I could do no good, when a few inquiries on the part of Mr. Taylor, inspired by a degree of curiosity or of anxiety, caused a few moments' delay, during which a lady by the name of Walton entered the house, and, being an acquaintance of Mrs. Taylor's, was soon engaged in conversation with her in an adjoining room. I overheard the following:

"Mrs. Walton, I am glad to see you; there is a gentleman here from the United States who says the Lord sent him to this city to preach the gospel. He has applied in vain to the clergy and to the various authorities for opportunity to fulfil his mission, and is now about to leave the place. He may be a man of God; I am sorry to have him depart."

"Indeed!" said the lady; "well, I now understand the feelings and spirit which brought me to your house at this time. I have been busy over the wash tub and too weary to take a walk; but I felt impressed to walk out. I then thought I would make a call on my sister, the other side of town; but passing your door, the Spirit bade me go in; but I said to myself, I will go in when I return; but the Spirit said: 'go in now.' I accordingly came in, and I am thankful that I did so. Tell the stranger he is welcome to my house. I am a widow; but I have a spare room and bed, and food in plenty. He shall have a home at my house, and two large rooms to preach in just when he pleases. Tell him I will send my son John over to pilot him to my house, while I go and gather my relatives and friends to come in this very evening and hear him talk; for I feel by the Spirit that he is a man sent by the Lord with a message which will do us good."

The evening found me quietly seated at her house, in the midst of a number of listeners, who were seated around a large work table in her parlor, and deeply interested in the conversation. . . .

After conversing with these interesting persons till a late hour, we retired to rest. Next day Mrs. Walton requested me to call on a friend of hers, who was also a widow in deep affliction, being totally blind with inflammation in the eyes; she had suffered extreme pain for several months, and had also been reduced to want, having four little children to support. She had lost her husband, of cholera, two years before, and had sustained herself and family by teaching school until deprived of sight, since which she had been dependent on the Methodist society; herself and children being then a public charge. Mrs. Walton sent her little daughter of twelve years old to show me the way. I called on the poor blind widow and helpless orphans, and found them in a dark and gloomy apartment, rendered more so by having every ray of light obscured to prevent its painful effects on her eyes. I related to her the circumstances of my mission, and she believed the same. I laid my hands upon her in the name of Jesus Christ, and said unto her, "your eyes shall be well from this very hour." She threw off her bandages; opened her house to the light; dressed herself, and walking with open eyes, came to the meeting that same evening at sister Walton's, with eyes as well and as bright as any other person's. (*Autobiography of Parley Parker Pratt*, reprint ed. [Salt Lake City: Deseret Book Co., 1976], pp. 135–38.)

The Gates of Hell
Will Not Prevail

Matthew 16:13–19

"When Jesus came into the coasts of Caesarea Philippi, he asked his disciples, saying, Whom do men say that I the Son of man am?

"And they said, Some say that thou art John the Baptist: some, Elias; and others, Jeremias, or one of the prophets.

"He saith unto them, But whom say ye that I am?

"And Simon Peter answered and said, Thou art the Christ, the Son of the living God.

"And Jesus answered and said unto him, Blessed art thou, Simon Bar-jona: for flesh and blood hath not revealed it unto thee, but my Father which is in heaven.

"And I say also unto thee, . . . upon this rock I will build my church; and the gates of hell shall not prevail against it.

"And I will give unto thee the keys of the kingdom of heaven: and whatsoever thou shalt bind on earth shall be bound in heaven: and whatsoever thou shalt loose on earth shall be loosed in heaven." (Matthew 16:13–19.)

The First Presidency Holds the Keys
to Receive Revelation for the Church

Elder Bruce R. McConkie said:

The gates of hell are the entrances to the benighted realms of the damned where the wicked go to await the day when they shall come forth in the resurrection of damnation. Those beckoning gates prevail against all who pass through them. But those who obey the laws and ordinances of the gospel have the promise that the gates of hell shall not prevail against them. (D&C 10:69; 17:8; 21:4–6; 98:22.) In this instance, *Jesus is telling Peter that the gates of hell shall never prevail against the rock of revelation;* that is, as long as the saints are living in righteousness so as to receive revelation from heaven, they will avoid the gates of hell and the Church itself will remain pure, undefiled, and secure against every evil. But when, because of iniquity, revelation ceases, then the gates of hell prevail against the people and also against the organization of which they are members. (*Doctrinal New Testament Commentary* [Salt Lake City: Bookcraft, 1973], 1:388–89; italics in original.)

President Harold B. Lee said:

When the Church was first organized, in fact, the day on which it was organized, the Lord was speaking to the Church. He didn't mean just the six members that were then the constituted number of the Church: he was speaking about the President of the Church, who was the Prophet Joseph Smith at that time. And this is what he said:

"Wherefore, meaning the church, thou shalt give heed unto all his [the President's] words and commandments which he shall give unto you as he receiveth them, walking in all holiness before me;

"For his word ye shall receive, as if from mine own mouth, in all patience and faith.

"For by doing these things the gates of hell shall not prevail against you; yea, and the Lord God will disperse the powers of darkness from before you, and cause the heavens to shake for your good, and his name's glory." (D&C 21:4–6.) (In Conference Report, October 1970, p. 152.)

"You Cannot Destroy the Appointment of a Prophet"

"Brigham Young in his day was invited into a group of some of those who were trying to argue against that principle of unity. After he learned that they were trying to 'depose' as they said, the Prophet Joseph Smith, he stood before them and said something like this: 'You cannot destroy the appointment of a prophet of God, but you can cut the thread which binds you to a prophet of God and sink yourselves to hell.'" (Harold B. Lee, Conference Report, April 1950, p. 101.)

The Personal Example of President Marion G. Romney

In the political field where so much pressure is exerted on men to compromise ideals and principles for expediency, party workers early learned to admire Marion G. Romney's intense loyalty to his own conscience as well as to the advice of his Church leaders whose pronouncements on vital issues affecting the welfare of the nation he accepted as divinely inspired even though it frequently brought him into sharp conflict with leaders of his own political party. On one such occasion when Church leaders in a tersely worded editorial had denounced the trends of the political administration then in power, he confided in me something which it might be well if all loyal Church members in public life could emulate: "When I read that editorial," he told me, "I knew what I should do—but that wasn't enough. I knew that I must feel right about following the counsel of the Church leaders and know that they were right. That took a whole night on my knees to accomplish." (Harold B. Lee, "Marion G. Romney," *Improvement Era*, October 1962, p. 742.)

Payment Made in a Miraculous Manner

Matthew 17:24–27

"And when they were come to Capernaum, they that received tribute money came to Peter, and said, Doth not your master pay tribute?

"He saith, Yes. And when he was come into the house, Jesus prevented him, saying, What thinkest thou, Simon? of whom do the kings of the earth take custom or tribute? of their own children, or of strangers?

"Peter saith unto him, Of strangers. Jesus saith unto him, Then are the children free.

"Notwithstanding, lest we should offend them, go thou to the sea, and cast an hook, and take up the fish that first cometh up; and when thou hast opened his mouth, thou shalt find a piece of money: that take, and give unto them for me and thee." (Matthew 17:24–27.)

Money in the Catfish's Mouth

In the summer of 1833, the Latter-day Saints were banished from central Missouri because of their faith in the restored gospel. They were driven by bigoted mobs out of Jackson County to the north. As quickly as they could, these stalwart Saints, stripped of nearly all their earthly possessions, began crossing the Missouri River into Clay County.

Historian Ivan J. Barrett described the scene with these words:

Wagons and oxen, horses, boxes, chests, goods and provisions were ready to be moved onto the ferries which were continually plying the inky waters and carrying the Saints to the Clay County side. Makeshift shelters were improvised to protect the refugees from the cold rain and sleet. Some of the exiles had the good fortune to escape with their families intact, household goods and some provisions, while others had barely eluded the mobs with "the skin of their teeth." When night enveloped the Saints, the wilderness along the Missouri River presented the appearance of a camp meeting. Hundreds of people were seen scattered in every direction; some in tents, some in wigwams made of willows, and some in the open around their blazing fires, huddling together in a downpour of rain. Newel Knight, one of the victims of mobocracy, described the plight of the banished Saints:

"Thus homeless and without means of taking much to sustain them did the whole Church in Jackson County flee before the mob, and at night. Those who went to the river camped in the rain which poured down in torrents; the frail mother, the helpless infant, the sick and the dying, all alike without the means to shelter themselves from the storm." (Journal of Newel Knight, in *Scraps of Biography* [Salt Lake City: The *Juvenile Instructor* office, 1887], pp. 83–84.)

The cost of ferrying across the river was one dollar and a half a trip for families, wagons, good[s], and teams. A few families had not the price and were left to camp on the Jackson side in constant fear that the mob, learning that they had not left the county, would kill them. A few of the brethren decided to try and catch some fish in the hope of persuading the ferrymen to accept them in lieu of money. They put out their lines in the evening. When the lines were drawn up three small fish and a large catfish were attached to the hooks. How great was their astonishment when the catfish was opened and three bright silver dollars were found inside—just enough to take the teams, wagons, and families over to the Clay County side of the river. One of the number wrote, "This was considered a miracle, and caused great rejoicing among us." (Diary of Mary Elizabeth Rollins Lightner, pp. 10–11.) (Ivan J. Barrett, *Joseph Smith and the Restoration* [Provo, Utah: Brigham Young University Press, 1967], p. 187.)

"He Went Away Sorrowful"

Matthew 19:16–22

"And, behold, one came and said unto him, Good Master, what good thing shall I do, that I may have eternal life?

"And he said unto him, Why callest thou me good? there is none good but one, that is, God: but if thou wilt enter into life, keep the commandments.

"He saith unto him, Which? Jesus said, Thou shalt do no murder, Thou shalt not commit adultery, Thou shalt not steal, Thou shalt not bear false witness,

"Honour thy father and thy mother: and, Thou shalt love thy neighbour as thyself.

"The young man saith unto him, All these things have I kept from my youth up: what lack I yet?

"Jesus said unto him, If thou wilt be perfect, go and sell that thou hast, and give to the poor, and thou shalt have treasure in heaven: and come and follow me.

"But when the young man heard that saying, he went away sorrowful: for he had great possessions." (Matthew 19:16–22.)

He Was So Offended He Apostatized

The dedication of the Kirtland Temple on March 27, 1836, was a tremendous event. Some of the most memorable spiritual manifestations occurred on that Sunday afternoon. Everyone knew how important this day would be. There was a spirit of anticipation that prevailed over the hearts of the Saints. And on this day, hours before the doors of the temple were opened for the dedicatory services, a large crowd gathered in hopeful anticipation of the day's events. Joseph Smith estimated that by 7:00 A.M. more than five hundred Saints were gathered around the temple doors. Between 7:00 and 8:00 A.M. several church leaders arrived and entered the building, and then Joseph, with the assistance of others present, dedicated the pulpits and consecrated them to the Lord.

At eight o'clock, the doors were opened and the First Presidency ushered in and helped seat approximately eight-hundred visitors in the main hall of the temple. After every available seat had been filled, the temple doors were closed, leaving hundreds of others, including some who had sacrificed much of their time and wealth for the construction of the temple, outside. Realizing their disappointment, Joseph suggested that they hold a meeting in a nearby schoolhouse, but soon that was filled as well. It was decided that the dedicatory service would be repeated the following Thursday, March 31, allowing others to participate.

One of the individuals who was not able to get inside the Kirtland Temple that morning was Frazier Eaton. He had donated approximately seven hundred dollars for the temple, a huge amount of money considering the financial depression that was underway. He assumed that there would surely be a place for him that morning. But not having arrived early enough to be admitted before the auditorium filled, he was prohibited from entering. He was so offended he apostatized from the Church. (See *Journal of Discourses*, 11:9.)

Those who remained and attended the dedicatory sessions were richly rewarded. During the fifteen-week period from January 21 to May 1, the spiritual outpouring and blessings from the Lord were so great that one modern historian has written, "Probably more Latter-day Saints beheld visions and witnessed other unusual spiritual manifestations than during any other era in the history of the Church." (See Milton V. Backman, Jr., *The Heavens Resound* [Salt Lake City: Deseret Book Co., 1983], p. 285.)

Members of the Church saw heavenly messengers in at least ten different meetings, and at five of these gatherings different individuals testified that they had beheld the Savior himself. Many experienced visions, some prophesied, and others spoke in tongues. (Ibid.)

Forsaking All for the Lord

Matthew 19:29

"And every one that hath forsaken houses, or brethren, or sisters, or father, or mother, or wife, or children, or lands, for my name's sake, shall receive an hundredfold, and shall inherit everlasting life" (Matthew 19:29).

Catherine Spencer

Catherine Curtis Spencer died on the 12th of March, 1846, at Indian Creek, near Keosaqua, Iowa Territory, at the age of thirty-five years, wanting nine days.

In one month from the time of her departure from Illinois to the wilderness, she fell a victim to the cares and hardships of persecution. The youngest daughter of a numerous family, brought up in affluence and nurtured with fondness and peculiar care, as the favorite of her father's house, her slender yet healthy frame could not withstand the inclemency of the winter season, (the thermometer below zero for ten days). The change from warm rooms of brick and plastered walls, to that of mere canvas ceiling and roof, floored with snow and icy earth, was too much for her fragile form to endure. When, through unforeseen hindrances in traveling, there was no place where sleep could visit, or food suited to the demands of nature be administered to her or her six little children, from the age of thirteen and under, she would cheer her little innocents with the songs of Zion. The melody of her rare voice, like the harmony and confluence of many virtues in her mind, contributed on that memorable epoch of the Church, to render her the glory of her husband and the solace and joy of her children. . . .

Under the influence of a severe cold, she gradually wasted away, telling her children, from time to time, how she wanted them to live, and conduct themselves, when they should be-come motherless and pilgrims in a strange land. To her com-panion she would some times say, "I think you will have to give me up and let me go." As her little ones would often in-quire at the door of the wagon, "How is mamma? is she any better?" she would turn to her husband, who sat by her side endeavoring to keep the severities of rain and cold from her, with, "Oh you dear little children, how I do hope you may fall into kind hands when I am gone!" A night or two before she died she said to her husband, with unwonted animation, "A heavenly messenger has appeared to me tonight and told me that I had done and suffered enough, and that he had now come to convey me to a mansion of gold."

Soon after, she said she wished her husband to call her children and her friends to her bedside, that she might give them a parting kiss; which, being done, she said to her com-panion, "I love you more than ever, but you must let me go. I only want to live for your sake and that of our children." When asked if she had anything to say to her father's family, she replied emphatically, "Charge them to obey the gospel."

The rain continued so incessantly for many days and nights, that it was impossible to keep her bedding dry or com-fortable, and, for the first time she uttered a desire to be in a house. . . . Immediately a man by the name of Barnes, living not far from the camp, consented to have her brought to his house, where she died in peace with a smile upon her counte-nance, and a cordial pressure of her husband's hand. . . .

Though prepossessing in her manner, her confiding and generous mind always made permanent the friendship she once obtained. Her unceasing and dutiful bearing to her hus-band, and her matronly diligence in infusing the purest and loftiest virtues into the minds of her children, not only exem-plified the beautiful order of heaven, but made her domestic circle the greatest paradise of earth. Said a member of the

High Council after her death, one who had often observed her in the Temple of the Lord, where she loved to linger and feast on the joys of that holy place, "I never saw a countenance more inexpressibly serene and heavenly, than hers."

Her remains were conveyed to the City of Nauvoo, and there, after a few neighbors had wept and sung, "Come to me, will ye come to the Saints that have died," and expressed their condolence to the deeply affected husband, were buried in the solitude of the night by the side of her youngest child that had died near six months before.

The writer does not mourn for his dead as those without hope, knowing they are taken from many evils to come. He desires to dedicate the above faint sketch to his children, now in the wilderness, for the testimony of Jesus, lest time should obliterate from their young and tender minds the recollections of their mother's person, and some of her virtues; thereby would he perpetuate the memory of the just. He desires the prayers of all the Saints, for himself and his children; and may the blessings of Almighty God rest upon all who love our Lord Jesus Christ in sincerity. (As quoted in Preston Nibley, *Exodus to Greatness* [Salt Lake City: Deseret News Press, 1947], pp. 133–35.)

Shortly after Catherine died, and while camped in a shanty at Winter Quarters, Nebraska, President Brigham Young was impressed to call their father, Orson Spencer, on a mission. Orson accepted without hesitation and left immediately. While in New York he wrote a letter to President Brigham Young on 26 November 1846. He closed his letter in this way: "Don't forget to give a good piece of my love to six little orphan children, somewhat south of you on Main Street. I sometimes think of the lambs in a stormy day, because some of them had not very warm fleeces for cold weather. Tell them I am happy, and they must be too, and I will write them before I cross the Atlantic. . . . Your humble brother and humble servant in the Gospel, Orson Spencer." (*Exodus to Greatness*, p. 295.)

Catherine Roe

When I was 14 years of age, I was apprenticed to the bookbinding trade at the firm of John Fazakerley, bookbinders to the King.

This firm did all the bookbinding for the British Mission with headquarters in Liverpool. Here were bound the Book of Mormon, Doctrine and Covenants, and Pearl of Great Price.

I had sewn hundreds of these books before I met the missionaries. The mission headquarters had a small printing press on which they printed the tracts which the missionaries distributed, such as "Rays of Living Light" and the *Millennial Star*. The *Star*, as we called it for short, had to be folded to book size and mailed to the missionaries, and for this purpose they hired an apprentice from the company where I worked.

It was my good fortune to be chosen for this job, and through proofreading of the *Star*, I caught a glimpse of the gospel.

The missionaries invited me to attend the meetings, which I did, and I became very much interested and induced my sister to go to the meetings with me. When our parents discovered this, they became very angry and gave us our choice of the Mormon Church or our home. Our opposition and persecution at home became so great we were forced to leave.

Our parents were invited by the minister of the church to which we belonged, Rev. Bartlett, who worked with all his might, to persecute the missionaries by inciting mobs to break up street meetings, and attend the church meetings and disrupt them. Our persecution became so great that President Charles W. Penrose, who was president of the European Mission at this time [1908—Catherine Roe was now 19] thought it best for us to emigrate to Utah and made it possible for us to do so.

My sister, Margaret, and I were scheduled to sail on August 15, 1908, to America. Senator Reed Smoot was in England on Church business. He happened to be on the Liverpool landing stage at the same time as my sister and I. We introduced our parents to him, as they had come to see us off on our trip. It took us eight days to cross the ocean. When we arrived in Boston, much to our dismay, our whole company of 108 Latter-day Saints was held up for investigation. The shipping officials had received a written telegram telling them to stop the runaway Roe girls. This telegram was sent by the Rev. Bartlett and was signed "Father."

My father denied having anything to do with it, but said as long as it had been sent he would stand back of it. And so we were to be deported. We prayed constantly day and night and in the middle of the night, and this is how our prayers were answered.

Senator Reed Smoot sailed for America the week after we sailed, and while he was in the middle of the ocean he received a wireless from President Penrose in Liverpool advising him to go to Boston and intervene for the Roe girls. He arrived in Boston ten days after we had been confined to the detention home. He was able to testify to the shipping officials that we were not running away, that he had witnessed our parents and our brother bid us goodbye and Godspeed, and so we were released and allowed to continue our journey.

This was a very trying experience, but the passage of scripture which tells us that "everyone that has forsaken houses of brethren, or sisters, or father, or mother, or wife, or children, or lands, for my name's sake, shall receive an hundredfold, and shall inherit everlasting life" has always been a comfort to us. (Matthew 19:29.) (See *Laurel Manual* [Salt Lake City: The Church of Jesus Christ of Latter-day Saints, 1970], p. 99.)

The Faith of a Young Woman

This story was told by Elder N. Eldon Tanner:

A young girl and her family were being taught the gospel right here in this city [Salt Lake City, Utah] by a returned missionary who was serving as a stake missionary. After the family had heard the first two discussions, the father said, "We want nothing more to do with it."

But this girl, who was about eighteen years of age, believed what she heard, and she wanted to be baptized. Her father said, "You can't be baptized. If you want to be baptized, you will have to wait until you are of age."

She was telling her boyfriend about the gospel and what it meant to her. He got tired of listening to her. He said one night, "You will have to choose between me and the Church."

This hurt her badly. She loved this young man, but as they talked it over and she shed some tears, she said, "I am going to stay with the Church. I know it is true."

She went home and was very much upset. Her father saw she was upset and asked her what was troubling her. She said, "Oh, nothing, Dad."

He said, "My dear, I know there is something wrong. What is it?"

She told him what had happened. He said, "If the Church means that much to you, you may be baptized." Three weeks from then she was baptized.

And who do you think was there to see the baptism? Her father, her mother, and her boyfriend; and three weeks later they were baptized. (In Conference Report, October 1968, p. 104.)

"Out of the Mouth of Babes"

Matthew 21:15–16

"And when the chief priests and scribes saw the wonderful things that he did, and the children crying in the temple, and saying, Hosanna to the Son of David; they were sore displeased,

"And said unto him, Hearest thou what these say? And Jesus saith unto them, Yea; have ye never read, Out of the mouth of babes and sucklings thou hast perfected praise?" (Matthew 21:15–16.)

Even the Little Children

This Colesville branch was among the first organized by Joseph Smith, and constituted the first settlers of the members of the Church in Missouri. They had arrived late in the summer, and cut some hay for their cattle, sowed a little grain, and prepared some ground for cultivation, and were engaged during the fall and winter in building log cabins, etc. The winter was cold, and for some time about ten families lived in one log cabin, which was open and unfinished, while the frozen ground served for a floor. Our food consisted of beef and a little bread made of corn, which had been grated into coarse meal by rubbing the ears on a tin grater. This was rather an inconvenient way of living for a sick person; but it was for the gospel's sake, and all were very cheerful and happy.

We enjoyed many happy seasons in our prayer and other meetings, and the Spirit of the Lord was poured out upon us, and even on the little children, insomuch that many of eight, ten or twelve years of age spake, and prayed, and prophesied in our meetings and in our family worship. There was a spirit of peace and union, and love and good will manifested in this little Church in the wilderness, the memory of which will be ever dear to my heart. (*Autobiography of Parley P. Pratt,* reprint ed. [Salt Lake City: Deseret Book Co., 1976], pp. 71–72.)

The Ten Virgins

Matthew 25:1–10

Then shall the kingdom of heaven be likened unto ten virgins, which took their lamps, and went forth to meet the bridegroom.

And five of them were wise, and five were foolish.

They that were foolish took their lamps, and took no oil with them:

But the wise took oil in their vessels with their lamps.

While the bridegroom tarried, they all slumbered and slept.

And at midnight there was a cry made, Behold, the bridegroom cometh; go ye out to meet him.

Then all those virgins arose, and trimmed their lamps.

And the foolish said unto the wise, Give us of your oil; for our lamps are gone out.

But the wise answered, saying, Not so; lest there be not enough for us and you: but go ye rather to them that sell, and buy for yourselves.

And while they went to buy, the bridegroom came; and they that were ready went in with him to the marriage: and the door was shut. (Matthew 25:1–10.)

Marriage Customs at the Time of Christ

The following description of Middle Eastern marriage customs from George M. Mackie's *Bible Manners and Customs* gives some valuable insights into the parable of the ten virgins:

Oriental marriages usually take place in the evening. . . . The whole attention is turned to the public arrival of the bridegroom to receive the bride prepared for him and waiting in the house among her female attendants.

If we make allowance for some changes in detail caused by their rules as to the seclusion of women, the Moslem customs are those which help us most in trying to understand how marriages took place in Bible times. During the day the bride is conducted to the house of her future husband, and she is there assisted by her attendants in putting on the marriage robes and jewellery. During the evening, the women who have been invited congregate in the room where the bride sits in silence, and spend the time commenting on her appearance, complimenting the relatives, discussing various family matters, and partaking of sweetmeats and similar refreshments.

As the hours drag on their topics of conversation become exhausted, and some of them grow tired and fall asleep. There is nothing more to be done, and everything is in readiness for the reception of the bridegroom, when the cry is heard outside announcing his approach.

The bridegroom meanwhile is absent spending the day at the house of one of his relatives. There, soon after sunset, that is between seven and eight o'clock, his male friends begin to assemble. Their work for the day is over; they have taken a hasty supper, and dressed themselves, and have come to spend the evening with the bridegroom and then escort him home. The time is occupied with light refreshments, general conversation and the recitation of poetry in praise of the two families chiefly concerned and of the bridegroom in particular. After all have been courteously welcomed and their congratulations received, the bridegroom, about eleven o'clock, intimates his wish to set out. Flaming torches are then held aloft by special bearers, lit candles are handed at the door to each visitor as he goes out, and the procession sweeps slowly along towards the house where the bride and her female attendants are waiting. A great crowd has meanwhile assembled on the balconies, garden-walls, and flat roofs of the houses on each side of the road. It is always an impressive spectacle to watch the passage of such a brilliant retinue

under the starry stillness of an Oriental night. The illumina-
tion of the torches and candles not only makes the procession
itself a long winding array of moving lights, but throws into
sharp relief the white dresses and thronging faces of the spec-
tators seen against the somber walls and dark sky. The bridegroom is the center of interest. Voices are heard whispering,
"There he is! there he is!" From time to time women raise
their voices in the peculiar shrill, wavering shriek by which
joy is expressed at marriages and other times of family and
public rejoicing. The sound is heard at a great distance, and is
repeated by other voices in advance of the procession, and
thus intimation is given of the approach half an hour or more
before the marriage escort arrives. It was during this interval
that the foolish virgins hurried out in quest of oil for their
lamps. Along the route the throng becomes more dense, and
begins to move with the retinue bearing the lights. As the
house is approached the excitement increases, the bridegroom's pace is quickened, and the alarm is raised in louder
tones and more repeatedly, "He is coming, he is coming!"

Before he arrives, the maidens in waiting come forth with
lamps and candles a short distance to light up the entrance,
and do honour to the bridegroom and the group of relatives
and intimate friends around him. These pass into the final rejoicing and the marriage supper: the others who have dis-
charged their duty in accompanying him to the door, immediately disperse, and the door is shut.

Such is the simple incident in the earthly home that has
found such wonderful correspondences in the heavenly life.
The bridal procession has been taken into the house of
Parable, and there robed with beautiful vesture of spiritual
truth. (*Bible Manners and Customs* [n.p.: Fleming H. Revell
Co., 1898], pp. 123–26.)

Stewardship and Accountability

Matthew 25:14–46

For the kingdom of heaven is as a man travelling into a far country, who called his own servants, and delivered unto them his goods.

And unto one he gave five talents, to another two, and to another one; to every man according to his several ability; and straightway took his journey.

Then he that had received the five talents went and traded with the same, and made them other five talents.

And likewise he that had received two, he also gained other two.

But he that had received one went and digged in the earth, and hid his lord's money.

After a long time the lord of those servants cometh, and reckoneth with them.

And so he that had received five talents came and brought other five talents, saying, Lord, thou deliveredst unto me five talents: behold, I have gained beside them five talents more.

His lord said unto him, Well done, thou good and faithful servant: thou hast been faithful over a few things, I will make thee ruler over many things: enter thou into the joy of thy lord.

He also that had received two talents came and said, Lord, thou deliveredst unto me two talents: behold, I have gained two other talents beside them.

His lord said unto him, Well done, good and faithful servant; thou hast been faithful over a few things, I will make thee ruler over many things: enter thou into the joy of thy lord.

Then he which had received the one talent came and said, Lord, I knew thee that thou art an hard man, reaping where thou hast not sown, and gathering where thou hast not strawed:

And I was afraid, and went and hid thy talent in the earth: lo, there thou hast that is thine.

His lord answered and said unto him, Thou wicked and slothful servant, thou knewest that I reap where I sowed not, and gather where I have not strawed:

Thou oughtest therefore to have put my money to the exchangers, and then at my coming I should have received mine own with usury.

Take therefore the talent from him, and give it unto him which hath ten talents.

For unto every one that hath shall be given, and he shall have abundance: but from him that hath not shall be taken away even that which he hath.

And cast ye the unprofitable servant into outer darkness: there shall be weeping and gnashing of teeth.

When the Son of man shall come in his glory, and all the holy angels with him, then shall he sit upon the throne of his glory:

And before him shall be gathered all nations: and he shall separate them one from another, as a shepherd divideth his sheep from the goats:

And he shall set the sheep on his right hand, but the goats on the left.

Then shall the King say unto them on his right hand, Come, ye blessed of my Father, inherit the kingdom prepared for you from the foundation of the world:

For I was an hungred, and ye gave me meat: I was thirsty, and ye gave me drink: I was a stranger, and ye took me in:

Naked, and ye clothed me: I was sick, and ye visited me: I was in prison, and ye came unto me.

Then shall the righteous answer him, saying, Lord, when

saw we thee an hungred, and fed thee? or thirsty, and gave thee drink?

When saw we thee a stranger, and took thee in? or naked, and clothed thee?

Or when saw we thee sick, or in prison, and came unto thee?

And the King shall answer and say unto them, Verily I say unto you, Inasmuch as ye have done it unto one of the least of these my brethren, ye have done it unto me.

Then shall he say also unto them on the left hand, Depart from me, ye cursed, into everlasting fire, prepared for the devil and his angels:

For I was an hungred, and ye gave me no meat: I was thirsty, and ye gave me no drink:

I was a stranger, and ye took me not in: naked, and ye clothed me not: sick, and in prison, and ye visited me not.

Then shall they also answer him, saying, Lord, when saw we thee an hungred, or athirst, or a stranger, or naked, or sick, or in prison, and did not minister unto thee?

Then shall he answer them, saying, Verily I say unto you, Inasmuch as ye did it not to one of the least of these, ye did it not to me.

And these shall go away into everlasting punishment: but the righteous into life eternal. (Matthew 25:14–46.)

Accountability Report

President David O. McKay gave the following statement in 1965 to a group of Church employees:

Let me assure you, Brethren, that some day you will have a personal priesthood interview with the Savior himself. If you are interested, I will tell you the order in which he will ask you to account for your earthly responsibilities.

First, he will request an accountability report about your relationship with your wife. Have you actively been engaged in making her happy and ensuring that her needs have been met as an individual?

Second, he will want an accountability report about each of your children individually. He will not attempt to have this for simply a family stewardship but will request information about your relationship to each and every child.

Third, he will want to know what you personally have done with the talents you were given in the preexistence.

Fourth, he will want a summary of your activity in your Church assignments. He will not be necessarily interested in what assignments you have had, for in his eyes the home teacher and a mission president are probably equals, but he will request a summary of how you have been of service to your fellowman in your Church assignments.

Fifth, he will have no interest in how you earned your living but if you were honest in all your dealings.

Sixth, he will ask for an accountability on what you have done to contribute in a positive manner to your community, state, country, and the world. (As quoted in Stephen R. Covey, *The Divine Center* [Salt Lake City: Bookcraft, 1982], pp. 54–55.)

"Ye Have Done It unto Me"

Matthew 25:40

"And the King shall answer and say unto them, Verily I say unto you, Inasmuch as ye have done it unto one of the least of these my brethren, ye have done it unto me" (Matthew 25:40).

"I Knew You Would Know Me"

Ardeth G. Kapp, former Young Women general president, told this story:

A few years ago, as it was nearing Christmas, I found myself confronted with a very full schedule. The streets were crowded, my calendar was crowded, and my mind was crowded. There was so much to do and so little time. An invitation to give a brief Christmas message to the residents of a nursing home nearby was one activity I could check off rather quickly and then hurriedly move to the next appointment.

As I rushed past the receptionist at the door of the nursing home, I was ushered into a large room where I suddenly stopped. Life was moving at a different pace here, if it was moving at all. There were wheelchairs, bent shoulders, gray hair, tired eyes, and the impression of so little going on. I reviewed quickly in my mind the message I had planned to share and hoped that it would fit and lift some heart, or at least be appropriate for this occasion. It was warm in the room but, in spite of this fact, many of the elderly had knitted shawls draped over rounded shoulders and woolly slippers covering tired feet.

Following my message, one of the visitors, a granddaughter of one of the elderly, asked if I would have time to visit with her grandmother in her own private room for even a few moments. She made the comment, "She thinks she knows you," indicating perhaps that her grandmother's mind might also be tired. I agreed that I could take a few moments, and I followed behind as the younger woman helped this elderly sister down the narrow hall back to her room. This dear lady reached her bedside, then shuffled haltingly as she turned around, let go of her granddaughter, and dropped onto the side of her bed. She then raised her head so that I could look into her face. My eyes caught hers. "Sister Myrtle Dudley," I said, "you were my Primary teacher."

The wrinkles on her face formed a smile as she pulled on her granddaughter's jacket and said, "See, I told you she would know me."

I continued, "I remember when you used to lead the singing. You wore that wine-colored dress with the big sleeves that waved back and forth as you taught us the songs."

Again she pulled on her granddaughter's jacket. "I told you she would know me."

"Yes," I said, "and you made carrot juice for my mother when she was sick."

Then she asked, "Did you come all the way from Canada just to see me?"

"Oh, Sister Dudley," I said, "I have come a long way. It has been over forty years." She then reached out her arms and drew me close to her. I felt like a child once again, back in Primary, in the arms of my teacher who loved me.

Then she whispered in my ear, "I knew you would know me."

There in the arms of my Primary teacher the world stood still for a moment. The busy streets were forgotten. The crowded calendar was no longer pressing on my mind. The spirit of Christmas filled my soul. A small miracle was taking place, not because of what I brought but because of what I had received.

After a time, I reluctantly and thoughtfully left the presence of my Primary teacher and walked slowly back to my car. I sat there pondering while the snowflakes of the season fell gently on the windshield that was piling high with snow. It was the season of celebration for the birth of Jesus Christ, our Lord and Savior. It was he who asked us to love one another and to serve one another. He said to each of us, "Inasmuch as ye have done it unto one of the least of these my brethren, ye have done it unto me" (Matthew 25:40). (Ardeth G. Kapp, "That We May Prepare To Do Our Part," in Brigham Young University *1988–89 Devotional and Fireside Speeches* [Provo, Utah: University Publications, 1989], pp. 130–31.)

Bathe and Feed the Baby

Elder Bruce R. McConkie related an experience that was recorded in his father's journal about his grandmother's compassionate service and the confirmation she received that her actions were pleasing to the Lord:

Mother was president of the Moab Relief Society. J____ B____ [a nonmember who opposed the Church] had married a Mormon girl. They had several children; now they had a new baby. They were very poor and Mother was going day by day to care for the child and to take them baskets of food, etc. Mother herself was ill, and more than once was hardly able to get home after doing the work at the J____B____ home.

One day she returned home especially tired and weary. She slept in her chair. She dreamed she was bathing a baby which she discovered was the Christ Child. She thought, Oh, what a great honor to thus serve the very Christ! As she held the baby in her lap, she was all but overcome. She thought, who else has actually held the Christ Child? Unspeakable joy filled her whole being. She was aflame with the glory of the Lord. It seemed that the very marrow in her bones would melt. Her joy was so great it awakened her. As she awoke, these words were spoken to her, "Inasmuch as ye have done it unto one of the least of these my brethren, ye have done it unto me." ("Charity Which Never Faileth," *Relief Society Magazine*, March 1970, p. 169.)

The Atoning Sacrifice

Matthew 26:36–46; Mark 14:32–42; Luke 22:39–47; John 18:1–3

Each of the four Gospels contains an account of the Savior's agony and sacrifice in the Garden of Gethsemane. All four accounts bear the same witness, but each one adds details not found in the others.

Matthew

Then cometh Jesus with them unto a place called Gethsemane, and saith unto the disciples, Sit ye here, while I go and pray yonder.

And he took with him Peter and the two sons of Zebedee, and began to be sorrowful and very heavy.

Then saith he unto them, My soul is exceeding sorrowful, even unto death: tarry ye here, and watch with me.

And he went a little further, and fell on his face, and prayed, saying, O my Father, if it be possible, let this cup pass from me: nevertheless not as I will, but as thou wilt.

And he cometh unto the disciples, and findeth them asleep, and saith unto Peter, What, could ye not watch with me one hour?

Watch and pray, that ye enter not into temptation: the spirit indeed is willing, but the flesh is weak.

He went away again the second time, and prayed, saying, O my Father, if this cup may not pass away from me, except I drink it, thy will be done.

And he came and found them asleep again: for their eyes were heavy.

And he left them, and went away again, and prayed the third time, saying the same words.

Then cometh he to his disciples, and saith unto them, Sleep on now, and take your rest: behold, the hour is at hand, and the Son of man is betrayed into the hands of sinners.

Rise, let us be going: behold, he is at hand that doth betray me. (Matthew 26:36–46.)

Mark

And they came to a place which was named Gethsemane: and he saith to his disciples, Sit ye here, while I shall pray.

And he taketh with him Peter and James and John, and began to be sore amazed, and to be very heavy;

And saith unto them, My soul is exceeding sorrowful unto death: tarry ye here, and watch.

And he went forward a little, and fell on the ground, and prayed that, if it were possible, the hour might pass from him.

And he said, Abba, Father, all things are possible unto thee; take away this cup from me: nevertheless not what I will, but what thou wilt.

And he cometh, and findeth them sleeping, and saith unto Peter, Simon, sleepest thou? couldest not thou watch one hour?

Watch ye and pray, lest ye enter into temptation. The spirit truly is ready, but the flesh is weak.

And again he went away, and prayed, and spake the same words.

And when he returned, he found them asleep again, (for their eyes were heavy,) neither wist they what to answer him.

And he cometh the third time, and saith unto them, Sleep on now, and take your rest: it is enough, the hour is come; behold, the Son of man is betrayed into the hands of sinners.

Rise up, let us go; lo, he that betrayeth me is at hand. (Mark 14:32–42.)

Luke

And he came out, and went, as he was wont, to the mount of Olives; and his disciples also followed him.

And when he was at the place, he said unto them, Pray that ye enter not into temptation.

And he was withdrawn from them about a stone's cast, and kneeled down, and prayed,

Saying, Father, if thou be willing, remove this cup from me: nevertheless not my will, but thine, be done.

And there appeared an angel unto him from heaven, strengthening him.

And being in an agony he prayed more earnestly: and his sweat was as it were great drops of blood falling down to the ground.

And when he rose up from prayer, and was come to his disciples, he found them sleeping for sorrow,

And said unto them, Why sleep ye? rise and pray, lest ye enter into temptation.

And while he yet spake, behold a multitude, and he that was called Judas, one of the twelve, went before them, and drew near unto Jesus to kiss him. (Luke 22:39–47.)

John

When Jesus had spoken these words, he went forth with his disciples over the brook Cedron, where was a garden, into the which he entered, and his disciples.

And Judas also, which betrayed him, knew the place: for Jesus ofttimes resorted thither with his disciples.

Judas then, having received a band of men and officers from the chief priests and Pharisees, cometh thither with lanterns and torches and weapons. (John 18:1–3.)

Witness of the Savior's Agony

Elder Orson F. Whitney said:

Then came a marvelous manifestation, and admonition from a higher source, one impossible to ignore. It was a dream, or a vision in a dream, as I lay upon my bed in the little town of Columbia, Lancaster County, Pennsylvania. I seemed to be in the Garden of Gethsemane, a witness of the Savior's agony. I saw Him as plainly as I have seen anyone. Standing behind a tree in the foreground, I beheld Jesus, with Peter, James and John, as they came through a little wicket gate at my right. Leaving the three Apostles there, after telling them to kneel and pray, the Son of God passed over to the other side, where He also knelt and prayed. It was the same prayer with which all Bible readers are familiar: "Oh my Father, if it be possible, let this cup pass from me; nevertheless not as I will but as Thou wilt."

As He prayed the tears streamed down His face, which was toward me. I was so moved at the sight that I also wept, out of pure sympathy. My whole heart went out to Him; I loved Him with all my soul, and longed to be with Him as I longed for nothing else.

Presently He arose and walked to where those Apostles were kneeling—fast asleep! He shook them gently, awoke them, and in tone of tender reproach, untinctured by the least show of anger or impatience, asked them plaintively if they could not watch with Him one hour. There He was, with the awful weight of the world's sins upon His shoulders, with the pangs of every man, woman and child shooting through His sensitive soul—and they could not watch with Him one poor hour!

Returning to His place, He offered up the same prayer as before; then went back and again found them sleeping. Again He awoke them, readmonished them, and once more returned and prayed. Three times this occurred, until I was perfectly familiar with His appearance—face, form, and movements. He was of noble stature and majestic mien—not at all the weak, effeminate being that some painters have portrayed; but the very God that He was and is, as meek and humble as a little child.

All at once the circumstances seemed to change, the scene remaining just the same. Instead of before, it was now after the crucifixion, and the Savior, with the three Apostles, now stood together in a group at my left. They were about to depart and ascend to Heaven. I could endure it no longer. I ran from behind the tree, fell at His feet, clasped Him around the knees, and begged Him to take me with Him.

I shall never forget the kind and gentle manner in which He stooped, raised me up, and embraced me. It was so vivid, so real. I felt the very warmth of His body, as He held me in His arms and said in tenderest tones: "No, my son; these have finished their work; they can go with me; but you must stay and finish yours." Still I clung to Him. Gazing up into His face—for He was taller than I—I besought Him fervently: "Well, promise me that I will come to you at the last." Smiling sweetly, He said: "That will depend entirely upon yourself." I awoke with a sob in my throat, and it was morning. (Orson F. Whitney, "A Vision of Gethsemane," *Instructor*, February 1968, pp. 63, 68.)

Be a Blessing

Matthew 27:55, 61

"And many women were there beholding afar off, which followed Jesus from Galilee, ministering unto him: . . .
"And there was Mary Magdalene, and the other Mary, sitting over against the sepulchre." (Matthew 27:55, 61.)

Desire to Bless Others

Authors Alan K. Parrish and Susan Easton Black described the wonderful contributions women in early Church history have made and the tremendous blessing they have been in the lives of others:

> In Proverbs we read, "Her children arise up, and call her blessed; her husband also, and he praiseth her" (31:28). Why? It is because such women desire to be a blessing and an influence for good in the lives of others. During the time of Christ, "Many women were there beholding afar off, which followed Jesus from Galilee, ministering unto him" (Matthew 27:55). This care and concern continued even after the death of Jesus as women diligently watched by the sepulchre (Matthew 27:61).
>
> Women in the latter days who have had their heartfelt prayers answered, desire to bless the lives of others.
>
> The minutes of the Female Relief Society of Nauvoo, August 5, 1843, taken by Eliza R. Snow, record:

Sister Joshua Smith found many sick in the Fourth ward and some destitute, in want of things to eat, and to use. Went and visited Sister McEwan and Sister Modley, found them and their families in suffering want—they need attendance every day. Sister Mecham visited Nehimiah Harmon's, found them poor, sick, and distressed, and no bedding—nothing comfortable, entirely destitute. Sister Mecham and Sister Billings solicited donations for the same. Sister Anderson gave one pair of stockings—$ .25. Sister Farr a calico dress and cape. Sister B. Ames, a peck of onions, one pound of sugar. Sister Clayton gave fourteen pounds of flour—$ .52; Lydia Moore one shirt—$ .50; Margaret Moore one shawl. Eliza R. Snow, secretary. (By May of 1843 membership and attendance outgrew the brick store, and summer meetings convened in the Nauvoo grove and in the homes of the sisters.)

Elizabeth Ann Whitney and her husband, Newel, provided a three-day feast in their home for the poor of the Church. Of this event, Joseph Smith's history states:

Attended a sumptuous feast at Bishop Newel K. Whitney's. This feast was after the order of the Son of God—the lame, the halt, and the blind were invited, according to the instructions of the Savior.

As with the early Relief Society members and the wife of a bishop, women in our era desire to help and be an influence for good. Whether it is the quiet visiting of the sick, the nurturing of the young, or the listening to a confused teenager, a righteous woman is there. May these noble women continue to be blessed as they give their lives to follow the great Exemplar, Jesus Christ. (*The New Testament and the Latter-day Saints* [Orem, Utah: Randall Book Co., 1987], pp. 57–58.)

"I Am with You"

Matthew 28:20

"Lo, I am with you alway, even unto the end of the world" (Matthew 28:20).

Guided by the Lord

I well remember when I was seven years old, baptism seemed to be far away, as though it would never be my turn. I watched with a fever of excitement as several members of my Sunday School class were baptized and confirmed. They somehow seemed different to me after baptism, and very important.

At last summer came, and Sister Nielsen, our teacher, reminded the class that I was next. I could hardly believe the time had come. I was to be baptized on my birthday, the 24th of July—Pioneer Day among the Latter-day Saints. At the water's edge I was confirmed and promised that I would have the Holy Ghost as a constant companion. A feeling of happiness and contentment filled me.

But as the days melted into months, I began to feel with some disappointment that, for a constant companion, the Holy Ghost had been uncomfortably silent. At times I wondered if somehow I had failed to live up to my special promise and confirmation.

Then came the second summer after my baptism. I was ten, and large for my age. I could quickly complete my assigned tasks at home and escape to my grandmother's house on her farm some distance away. My feet seemed to have wings, and I flew the distance, anxious to be with the dearest person I knew.

It was haying time, and the men on the hay crew were already in the field as I hurried along my way. At grandmother's there would be long tables groaning under the weight of wonderful food: produce from the garden, fresh-baked bread, and berry pies.

The day seemed to fly by, as did all the special summer days spent with my grandmother. It was with great reluctance that I said good-bye and took my departure. As always, I hated to leave the happy warmth of my grandmother's pleasant kitchen, but I had seen the shadows lengthening over the trees and down the hill beyond her house. I knew if I delayed much longer it would grow dark before I reached home—an uneasy thought, even though I would be able to see the lighted windows of my home beckoning in the distance in the river valley below.

I sat a few moments on the step, savoring the sweet scent of the ripening fruit in the orchard and the roses trailing up and over the back porch. "Why does it have to get dark?" I thought.

With a sigh of resignation, I moved down the walk and through the garden gate. As I crossed the yard beyond and went through the gate on the hill, I realized with a start that night had fallen. Even the shadows had disappeared. I kicked some rocks as I made my way down the steep hill. I could hear them bounce all the way to the bottom. Usually it was fun to kick rocks down the hill, but tonight the sound they made seemed ominous as they disappeared into the night.

On reaching the bottom of the hill, I was brought up short, remembering that there were big ruts filled with water where many wagons had crossed during the day. I had jumped from rock to rock to cross when I came, but the darkness made that impossible now. "Oh well," I thought, "it's warm and my shoes are old anyway." I plunged across, slipping and sliding on the rocks and oozing mud.

The frogs that had been intoning with stentorious sound now grew silent, causing my fear to grow like a dark specter.

"I'll sing," I told myself, and launched into a song that I felt was designed especially for those who, like myself, grew faint of heart: "Onward Christian soldiers, marching as to war!"

The words were hardly out of my mouth when a voice in my mind said, "Be still, and listen."

For a moment I was startled, but then I thought it was foolishness and began to sing with more vigor still, "With the cross of Jesus marching on before," and marched to build my flagging courage.

This time my head filled with the command, "Be still, and listen!"

I stopped short, and my heartbeat seemed louder than the thud of my marching, squishy-wet shoes just moments before. Resolutely drawing a long breath, I began again, "Onward—" But before the words would come, more demanding than ever I heard, "Be still!"

I stopped. The last shred of courage disappeared as if it were a leaf caught in a whirlwind. What should I do? Terror gripped me from all sides, and I began to pray in my heart, "Heavenly Father, please bless me!" I couldn't even think what it was that I should ask for. Just over and over the prayer, "Heavenly Father, please bless me," until the flood of terror subsided and a sweet reassurance filled my being. Then I heard the words, "Get off the road!"

This time I obeyed at once, and as silently as I had been loud before, I walked, sensing rather than seeing my way. I covered a half-mile in the field adjacent to the road, swallowed up in a void of blackness. My breathing seemed suspended, and I was intent on the night sounds around me, some easily identified and others strange and labored.

The creek crossing was just ahead, and I thought at once of the gate nearby, and whether I should crawl over it or through the fence. Almost before the thought came the answer, "Don't cross at the gate."

Where should I cross, then? I paused again, this time to contemplate the thought of the creek and the boggy swamp with cattails and brush that followed its sides. It would be difficult enough in the daylight, but at night? . . .

Then I smelled an odor borne on the night air that brought terror and instant knowledge: the smell of tobacco smoke, acrid and penetrating! There was someone near the gate, and every strained nerve assured me that this presence was menacing.

How I crossed the swampy creek and gained the ground on the other side has long since passed from my memory. What is plain and very vivid in my mind is my arrival home and my explanation for the torn and disheveled condition I was in, and the circumstances surrounding it.

My father believed my words without question. He put on his boots, took down his shotgun, and set off in the darkness across the fields. He returned many hours later with no explanation but with the comforting assurance that I had most certainly done the right thing.

Although that marked the end of my long and pleasant evenings walking home in the dusk, I felt a happiness and gratitude for the knowledge that came to me that I indeed had the companionship of the Holy Ghost. How grateful I am for this knowledge, for it has served me well. I trust it will to the end of my life. Has not the Savior promised, "And, lo, I am with you alway, even unto the end of the world" (Matt. 28:20)? (Cherie B. Warnock, "Lo, I Am with You," *Ensign*, February 1985, pp. 61–62.)

He Commands Unclean Spirits with Authority

Mark 1:23–27

"And there was in their synagogue a man with an unclean spirit; and he cried out,

"Saying, Let us alone; what have we to do with thee, thou Jesus of Nazareth? art thou come to destroy us? I know thee who thou art, the Holy One of God.

"And Jesus rebuked him, saying, Hold thy peace, and come out of him.

"And when the unclean spirit had torn him, and cried with a loud voice, he came out of him.

"And they were all amazed, insomuch that they questioned among themselves, saying, What thing is this? what new doctrine is this? for with authority commandeth he even the unclean spirits, and they do obey him." (Mark 1:23–27.)

"I Have More Authority Than You"

Elder Charles S. Hyde related this experience in the April 1926 general conference:

> I believe I realize to a certain extent the feeling experienced by some of the Seventies in the time of Christ when they returned from their missions, and with joy reported that

even the evil spirits had been subjected unto them by the name of Christ. I have also had a similar experience, when even the evil spirits have been subject unto us through the name of Christ. We had one in the [Netherlands] mission field afflicted with an evil spirit, and his body tormented and tortured by the possession of that evil spirit. I came into the room upon one occasion, and the evil spirit sprang upon me and seized me by the throat with a grip of iron, shutting off even my ability to speak and almost to breathe, while the elders stood round about, also my wife with a feeling of fear in her heart that the evil spirit would overcome me. He shouted with a voice that was most terrific. He declared himself to be the devil. "My name is Satan," he declared, "and I have more authority than you." And again tightening his grip upon my throat he declared, "I have more authority than you." I could not speak, but I looked the person in the eye, and releasing his grip and falling upon the bed, that same voice declared, "No, I have not more authority," and he hid his face in the pillow and was subject to the power of the Priesthood. Elder Kooyman, who was conference president, anointed him with oil, and with other elders I laid my hands upon him, and I began to confirm the anointing with oil. When I reached the point in prayer, that "in the name of Jesus Christ," I was going to say, "we rebuke the spirit," he sprang from the bed, and pleaded: "Do not use that name, do not use that name." We placed him upon the bed, and in the name of Jesus Christ I rebuked that spirit and commanded it to depart from him, and the person who was afflicted fell limp upon the bed and slept for hours, the first peaceful sleep he had enjoyed for several days. One of the greatest witnesses that have come into my life was upon this occasion. (In Conference Report, April 1926, p. 125.)

Arise and Walk!

Mark 2:1-12

And again he entered into Capernaum after some days; and it was noised that he was in the house.

And straightway many were gathered together, insomuch that there was no room to receive them, no, not so much as about the door: and he preached the word unto them.

And they come unto him, bringing one sick of the palsy, which was borne of four.

And when they could not come nigh unto him for the press, they uncovered the roof where he was: and when they had broken it up, they let down the bed wherein the sick of the palsy lay.

When Jesus saw their faith, he said unto the sick of the palsy, Son, thy sins be forgiven thee.

But there were certain of the scribes sitting there, and reasoning in their hearts,

Why doth this man thus speak blasphemies? who can forgive sins but God only?

And immediately when Jesus perceived in his spirit that they so reasoned within themselves, he said unto them, Why reason ye these things in your hearts?

Whether is it easier to say to the sick of the palsy, Thy sins be forgiven thee; or to say, Arise, and take up thy bed, and walk?

But that ye may know that the Son of man hath power on earth to forgive sins, (he saith to the sick of the palsy,)

I say unto thee, Arise, and take up thy bed, and go thy way into thine house.

And immediately he arose, took up the bed, and went forth before them all; insomuch that they were all amazed, and glorified God, saying, We never saw it on this fashion. (Mark 2:1–12.)

Gift of Healing

President Wilford Woodruff wrote the following:

Before starting on our missions to England, we were under the necessity of settling our families. A place called Commerce, afterwards named Nauvoo, was selected as the place at which our people should settle.

I left Quincy, in company with Brother Brigham Young and our families on the 15th of May, and arrived in Commerce on the 18th. After an interview with Joseph we crossed the river at Montrose, Iowa. President Brigham Young and myself, with our families, occupied one room about fourteen feet square. Finally Brother Young obtained another room and moved his family into it. Then Brother Orson Pratt and family moved into the same room with myself and family. . . .

While I was living in this cabin in the old barracks, we experienced a day of God's power with the Prophet Joseph. It was a very sickly time and Joseph had given up his home in Commerce to the sick, and had a tent pitched in his dooryard and was living in that himself. The large number of Saints who had been driven out of Missouri, were flocking into Commerce; but had no homes to go into, and were living in wagons, in tents, and on the ground. Many, therefore, were sick through the exposure they were subjected to. Brother Joseph had waited on the sick, until he was worn out and nearly sick himself.

On the morning of the 22nd of July, 1839, he arose, reflecting upon the situation of the Saints of God in their persecutions and afflictions, and he called upon the Lord in prayer, and the power of God rested upon him mightily, and as Jesus healed all the sick around Him in His day, so Joseph, the Prophet of God, healed all around on this occasion. He healed all in his house and door-yard, then, in company with

Sidney Rigdon and several of the Twelve, he went among the sick lying on the bank of the river and he commanded them in a loud voice, in the name of Jesus Christ, to come up and be made whole, and they were all healed. When he healed all that were sick on the east side of the river, they crossed the Mississippi river in a ferry-boat to the west side, to Montrose, where we were. The first house they went into was President Brigham Young's. He was sick on his bed at the time. The Prophet went into his house and healed him, and they all came out together. As they were passing by my door, Brother Joseph said: "Brother Woodruff, follow me." These were the only words spoken by any of the company from the time they left Brother Brigham's house till we crossed the public square, and entered Brother Fordham's house. Brother Fordham had been dying for an hour, and we expected each minute would be his last.

I felt the power of God that was overwhelming His Prophet.

When we entered the house, Brother Joseph walked up to Brother Fordham, and took him by the right hand; in his left hand he held his hat.

He saw that Brother Fordham's eyes were glazed, and that he was speechless and unconscious.

After taking hold of his hand, he looked down into the dying man's face and said: "Brother Fordham, do you not know me?" At first he made no reply; but we could all see the effect of the Spirit of God resting upon him.

He again said: "Elijah, do you not know me?"

With a low whisper, Brother Fordham answered, "Yes!"

The Prophet then said, "Have you not faith to be healed?"

The answer, which was a little plainer than before, was: "I am afraid it is too late. If you had come sooner, I think I might have been."

He had the appearance of a man waking from sleep. It was the sleep of death.

Joseph then said: "Do you believe that Jesus is the Christ?"

"I do, Brother Joseph," was the response.

Then the Prophet of God spoke with a loud voice, as in the majesty of the Godhead: "Elijah, I command you, in the name of the Jesus of Nazareth, to arise and be made whole!"

The words of the Prophet were not like the words of man, but like the voice of God. It seemed to me that the house shook from its foundation.

Elijah Fordham leaped from his bed like a man raised from the dead. A healthy color came to his face, and life was manifested in every act.

. . . [He] then called for his clothes and put them on. He asked for a bowl of bread and milk, and ate it; then put on his hat and followed us into the street, to visit others who were sick. . . .

As soon as we left Brother Fordham's house, we went into the house of Joseph B. Noble, who was very low and dangerously sick.

When we entered the house, Brother Joseph took him by the hand, and commanded him, in the name of Jesus Christ, to arise and be made whole. He did arise and was immediately healed. . . .

This case of Brother Noble's was the last one of healing upon that day. It was the greatest day for the manifestation of the power of God through the gift of healing since the organization of the Church.

When we left Brother Noble, the Prophet Joseph went with those who accompanied him from the other side, to the banks of the river, to return home.

While waiting for the ferry-boat, a man of the world, knowing of the miracles which had been performed, came to him and asked him if he would not go and heal two twin children of his, about five months old, who were both lying sick nigh unto death.

They were some two miles from Montrose.

The Prophet said he could not go; but, after pausing some time, he said he would send someone to heal them; and he turned to me and said: "You go with the man and heal his children.". . .

I went with the man, and did as the Prophet commanded me, and the children were healed. (Wilford Woodruff, *Leaves from My Journal,* in *Three Mormon Classics,* comp. Preston Nibley [Salt Lake City: Bookcraft, 1988], pp. 74–79.)

"Be Not Afraid,
Only Believe"

Mark 5:22–23, 35–43

And, behold, there cometh one of the rulers of the synagogue, Jairus by name; and when he saw him, he fell at his feet,

And besought him greatly, saying, My little daughter lieth at the point of death: I pray thee, come and lay thy hands on her, that she may be healed; and she shall live. . . .

While he yet spake, there came from the ruler of the synagogue's house certain which said, Thy daughter is dead: why troublest thou the Master any further?

As soon as Jesus heard the word that was spoken, he saith unto the ruler of the synagogue, Be not afraid, only believe.

And he suffered no man to follow him, save Peter, and James, and John the brother of James.

And he cometh to the house of the ruler of the synagogue, and seeth the tumult, and them that wept and wailed greatly.

And when he was come in, he saith unto them, Why make ye this ado, and weep? the damsel is not dead, but sleepeth.

And they laughed him to scorn. But when he had put them all out, he taketh the father and the mother of the damsel, and them that were with him, and entereth in where the damsel was lying.

And he took the damsel by the hand, and said unto her, Talitha cumi; which is, being interpreted, Damsel, I say unto thee, arise.

And straightway the damsel arose, and walked; for she was of the age of twelve years. And they were astonished with a great astonishment.

And he charged them straitly that no man should know it; and commanded that something should be given her to eat. (Mark 5:22–23, 35–43.)

Come Back and Live

A member of the Church in Brigham City, Ella Jensen, lingered for many weeks between life and death. She finally succumbed to scarlet fever. Her father, Jacob Jensen, knowing that President Lorenzo Snow was at a meeting in the Brigham City Tabernacle, went to visit the prophet. He later wrote, "I went into the vestry, behind the main hall, wrote a note and had it sent to [President Snow], who was speaking to the congregation. When the note was placed upon the pulpit, President Snow stopped his talking, read the note and then explained to the Saints that it was a call to visit some people who were in deep sorrow and asked to be excused."

The prophet and the stake president, Rudger Clawson, hurried to Ella's bedside. She had been dead about two hours. President Clawson wrote of their experience:

As we entered the home we met Sister Jensen, who was very much agitated and alarmed. We came to Ella's bedside and were impressed by the thought that her spirit had passed out of the body and gone beyond.

Turning to me President Snow said: "Brother Clawson, will you anoint her," which I did. We then laid our hands upon her head and the anointing was confirmed by President Snow, who blessed her and among other things, used this very extraordinary expression, in a commanding tone of voice, "Come back, Ella, come back. Your work upon the earth is not yet completed, come back." Shortly afterward we left the home.

Ella's father described what happened: "Ella remained in this condition for more than an hour after President Snow administered to her, or more than three hours in all after she died. We were sitting there watching by the bedside, her mother and my-self, when all at once she opened her eyes. She looked about the room, saw us sitting there, but still looked for someone else, and the first thing she said was: 'Where is he? Where is he?' We asked, 'Who? Where is who?' 'Why, Brother Snow,' she replied. 'He called me back.'"

Ella not only recovered, she also married and became the mother of eight children. (Leroi C. Snow, "Raised from the Dead," *Improvement Era*, September 1929, pp. 881–86; October 1929, p. 980.)

Get the Best Medical and Spiritual Help Available

There must be a certain necessary preparation before you can receive these divine communications. The Lord expects you and me to seek and to knock and to do and to keep his commandments if we would know, and to do all we can that lies within our power before we seek spiritual help. I remember, to illustrate what I mean, a sister coming to my office some years ago. She was an elderly sister and was troubled now with a serious heart ailment. Her children had urged her to go to a doctor and the doctor had prescribed some kind of heart stimulant, I suppose digitalis, or something akin to it. But she had resisted the idea, she said, "I have the faith that if I can receive a blessing I won't need any medicine." And so she had come to me to stand out against the doctor and her family and make it unnecessary for her to be so treated. I said I would like to read you something that Brigham Young said. He came to a home of some people who were ill, they were troubled with some kind of an intestinal disorder. He said to the mother, "Have you taken any herbs?" I suppose referring to a pioneer remedy that was common for use in such an ail-ment. And she replied, "Oh, no, Brother Brigham, I have the faith that if you just lay your hands upon my head I won't need any herbs or any medicine." And for an answer he pointed out through the window to a vacant piece of property and he said something like this, "You might just as well expect the Lord to cause wheat and corn to grow on that bare ground without you ever plowing or planting as to expect the Lord to do something for you that you know what to do for yourself without you putting first the effort." "But," he said, "I have the faith that if we were traveling in the mountains and all we could get was a little venison and we had some ailment then we could ask the Lord to do everything because there was nothing we could do for ourselves. And it is my faith that he could and would perform a miracle in our behalf." (Harold B. Lee, *But Arise and Stand upon Thy Feet—And I Will Speak with Thee*, Brigham Young University Speeches of the Year [Provo, 7 February 1956], pp. 5–6.)

"Because of Their Unbelief"

Mark 6:5–6

"And [Jesus] could there do no mighty work, save that he laid his hands upon a few sick folk, and healed them.

"And he marvelled because of their unbelief. And he went round about the villages, teaching." (Mark 6:5–6.)

"We Won't Give Up Our Hating!"

During visits to war-torn Europe with Elder Ezra Taft Benson, Frederick Babbel gives the following account of a blessing given:

The second person was a three-year-old boy from Scotland. He had been a deaf mute since birth. Now his parents had brought him to London for a special blessing. One of the brethren anointed his head with oil, and as I placed my hands upon his head to seal the anointing and to give him a blessing, I felt that the Lord's power was present in such abundance that there was no question about his being healed instantly.

Before I could say a word, I was told by the Spirit, "This young boy could be healed this very night if his parents would lose the hatred which they have in their hearts." I was decidedly shocked and troubled, because I had never before met this family and did not want to question their attitude. But I was restrained from sealing the anointing.

After a moment's pause, I removed my hands from the boy's head and said to his parents, "What is it that you hate so deeply?"

They looked startled. Then the husband said, "We can't tell you."

"I don't need to know," I replied, "but as I placed my hands upon your son's head, I was assured that he might be healed this very night and be restored to you whole if you will only lose the hatred which you have in your hearts."

After some troubled glances back and forth between the couple, the husband again spoke. "Well, if that is the case," he said, "our son will have to go through life as he is, because we won't give up our hating!"

I felt that I had been prevented from pronouncing a blessing that might have resulted in the salvation of the entire family. (Frederick W. Babbel, *On Wings of Faith*, [Salt Lake City: Bookcraft, 1972], pp. 160–61.)

"It Shall Not Hurt Them"

Mark 16:17–18

"And these signs shall follow them that believe; In my name shall they cast out devils; they shall speak with new tongues;

"They shall take up serpents; and if they drink any deadly thing, it shall not hurt them: they shall lay hands on the sick, and they shall recover." (Mark 16:17–18.)

Unharmed by Serpents

President Wilford Woodruff wrote:

> In the early days of the Church, it was a great treat to an Elder in his travels through the country to find a "Mormon"; it was so with us. We were hardly in Arkansas when we heard of a family named Akeman. They were in Jackson County in the persecutions. Some of the sons had been tied up there and whipped on their bare backs with hickory switches by the mob. We heard of their living on Petit Jean River, in the Arkansas Territory, and we went a long way to visit them . . . .
>
> We arrived . . . within five miles of Mr. Akeman's and were kindly entertained by a stranger. During the night I had the following dream:
>
> I thought an angel came to us, and told us we were commanded of the Lord to follow a certain straight path, which was pointed out to us, let it lead us wherever it might. After we had walked in it awhile we came to the door of a house,

which was in the line of a high wall running north and south, so that we could not go around. I opened the door and saw the room was filled with large serpents, and I shuddered at the sight. My companion said he would not go into the room for fear of the serpents. I told him I should try to go through the room though they killed me, for the Lord had commanded it. As I stepped into the room, the serpents coiled themselves up, and raised their heads some two feet from the floor, to spring at me. There was one much larger than the rest in the center of the room, which raised its head nearly as high as mine and made a spring at me. At that instant I felt as though nothing but the power of God could save me, and I stood still. Just before the serpent reached me he dropped dead at my feet; all the rest dropped dead, swelled up, turned black, burst open, took fire and were consumed before my eyes, and we went through the room unharmed, and thanked God for our deliverance.

I awoke in the morning and pondered upon the dream. We took breakfast, and started on our journey on Sunday morning, to visit Mr. Akeman. I related to my companion my dream, and told him we should see something strange. We had great anticipations of meeting Mr. Akeman, supposing him to be a member of the Church. When we arrived at his house, he received us very coldly, and we soon found that he had apostatized. He brought railing accusations against the Book of Mormon and the authorities of the Church.

Word was sent through all the settlements on the river for twenty miles that two "Mormon" preachers were in the place. A mob was soon raised, and warning sent to us to leave immediately or we would be tarred and feathered, ridden on a rail and hanged. I soon saw where the serpents were. My companion wanted to leave; I told him no, I would stay and see my dream fulfilled.

There was an old gentleman and lady, named Hubbel, who had read the Book of Mormon and believed. Father Hubbel came to see us, and invited us to make our home with him while we stayed in the place. We did so, and labored for him some three weeks with our axes, clearing land, while we were waiting to see the salvation of God.

I was commanded of the Lord by the Holy Ghost to go and warn Mr. Akeman to repent of his wickedness. I did so, and each time he railed against me, and the last time he ordered me out of his house. When I went out he followed me, and was very angry. When he came up to me, about eight rods from the house, he fell dead at my feet, turned black and swelled up, as I saw the serpents do in my dream.

His family, as well as ourselves, felt it was the judgment of God upon him. I preached his funeral sermon. Many of the mob died suddenly. We stayed about two weeks after Akeman's death and preached, baptized Mr. Hubbel and his wife, and then continued on our journey. (*Leaves from My Journal*, in *Three Mormon Classics*, comp. Preston Nibley [Salt Lake City: Bookcraft, 1988], pp. 18–20.)

"Whereby Shall I Know This?"

Luke 1:5–22

There was in the days of Herod, the king of Judaea, a certain priest named Zacharias, of the course of Abia: and his wife was of the daughters of Aaron, and her name was Elisabeth.

And they were both righteous before God, walking in all the commandments and ordinances of the Lord blameless.

And they had no child, because that Elisabeth was barren, and they both were now well stricken in years.

And it came to pass, that while he executed the priest's office before God in the order of his course,

According to the custom of the priest's office, his lot was to burn incense when he went into the temple of the Lord.

And the whole multitude of the people were praying without at the time of incense.

And there appeared unto him an angel of the Lord standing on the right side of the altar of incense.

And when Zacharias saw him, he was troubled, and fear fell upon him.

But the angel said unto him, Fear not, Zacharias: for thy prayer is heard; and thy wife Elisabeth shall bear thee a son, and thou shalt call his name John.

And thou shalt have joy and gladness; and many shall rejoice at his birth.

For he shall be great in the sight of the Lord, and shall drink neither wine nor strong drink; and he shall be filled with the Holy Ghost, even from his mother's womb.

And many of the children of Israel shall he turn to the Lord their God.

And he shall go before him in the spirit and power of Elias, to turn the hearts of the fathers to the children, and the disobedient to the wisdom of the just; to make ready a people prepared for the Lord.

And Zacharias said unto the angel, Whereby shall I know this? for I am an old man, and my wife well stricken in years.

And the angel answering said unto him, I am Gabriel, that stand in the presence of God; and am sent to speak unto thee, and to shew thee these glad tidings.

And, behold, thou shalt be dumb, and not able to speak, until the day that these things shall be performed, because thou believest not my words, which shall be fulfilled in their season.

And the people waited for Zacharias, and marvelled that he tarried so long in the temple.

And when he came out, he could not speak unto them: and they perceived that he had seen a vision in the temple: for he beckoned unto them, and remained speechless. (Luke 1:5–22.)

Faith in the Words of Heavenly Messengers

While serving a mission in the southern states, Elder Brigham H. Roberts had a remarkable experience, that helps us appreciate better the situation of Zacharias:

[Elder Roberts] had followed his previous strategy, spread his map out, prayed, considered several small towns, and then "as a result of my own judgment strictly, not of any inspiration" decided to go to Mason City. A fine Catholic family named Slade had been lodging him and had generously given him aid. On the night before his planned departure for Mason City he slept on a lounge bed in the parlor of the Slade home.

"As the day was dawning I began to wake and found myself with my face turned closely to the wall, somewhat cramped from lying too long in one position. I stretched and turned over on the other side, facing now the spacious sitting room.

"To my astonishment as I looked down upon the carpet I saw the bare feet of a personage. Gradually I looked up until the whole figure was before me. I saw standing there a young man, medium-sized, beardless, and light-complexioned. I noticed beautifully wavy hair, tastefully waved about a handsome face. This personage was truly noble in his bearing; erect, but not stiff, a graceful subtle pose which seemed so quiet and native to him. I looked upon him for some moments, the shock passing , and a beautiful feeling of confidence and pleasure clothed the circumstance. Then the youth bent forward smiling and slowly and gracefully raising his hand he pointed to the eastward and said in a voice, the tenderness and beauty of which can never be forgotten, 'You are called to go to Rockford.' Then gradually the vision vanished. . . ."

[Elder] Roberts . . . arose, dressed, and walked out on the open prairie in the long grass and wild flowers. The dew was heavy enough that on his return his feet were wet. It was a "pondering walk"; "My mind was perplexed," he records. "Had I not made up my mind to go to Mason City? Had I not told the whole neighborhood I was going there? To change my mind now, would they not regard me as fickle-minded? Besides, I did not like giving up my own arrangements." These statements, given in an article for youth under the title "Fruits of Disobedience," may overstate his willfulness. But earlier notes likewise record that he vacillated back and forth. And under such circumstances, he admits that even vacillating was "very unusual."

Neither Roberts nor the Slades had ever heard of Rockford. But at the breakfast table a hired man said that his parents lived there. It was a town to the northeast. "I said no more to them and decided at last to carry out my own plans at all hazards." Accordingly Roberts set out for Mason City, despite the message he had received, and faced an unbroken series of insults, cold shoulders and slammed doors. He was "sternly refused" meetinghouses and schools in Mason City, and met instant enmity in every attempt at communication. Hoping for a better reception on the outskirts of the city, he failed again. He resolved to try more remote rural areas, trudging for hours in the August sun with his grip becoming heavier in his hands. At one home where the table was laded with food he was invited in. But as soon as he was introduced to the head of the home, seated at table, the man said, "with cold severe tones": "then you are a Mormon preacher . . . the sooner you get out of my house the better." "I have come with an important message," Roberts replied. The man roughly ordered Roberts to leave.

After several more rebuffs and misdirections the sun set and the weary elder soliloquized, "Well it looks as if I might spend another night in the open prairie," and he laid down in "as good a place as any."

"Soon I discovered that the grass was full of spiders and bugs. From my grip I took a large handkerchief, wound it around my head, and began to fight for rest with crickets, insects and vermin. For when I next became conscious the sun was struggling through the mist to shine in my face. [Elsewhere he says the sun was an hour high before he awoke.] Rising to a sitting posture, my knees drawn up and hands over my knees, I began to review my experiences of the past few days and then commented, 'Well, this is a pretty hard way, it seems to me, to serve the Lord!' Just then, as if in answer to my comment, the severe and clear reproving voice, evidently of the one who visited me in the Slade living room, spoke out, 'You were told to go to Rockford.' Leaping like lightning, I turned in the direction of the voice and cried out aloud, 'So I was and to Rockford I will go! I've had enough of this.'" (Truman G. Madsen, *Defender of the Faith: The B.H. Roberts Story* [Salt Lake City: Bookcraft, 1980], pp. 115–17.)

"Get Thee Behind Me"

Luke 4:1–8

And Jesus being full of the Holy Ghost returned from Jordan, and was led by the Spirit into the wilderness,

Being forty days tempted of the devil. And in those days he did eat nothing: and when they were ended, he afterward hungered.

And the devil said unto him, If thou be the Son of God, command this stone that it be made bread.

And Jesus answered him, saying, It is written, That man shall not live by bread alone, but by every word of God.

And the devil, taking him up into an high mountain, shewed unto him all the kingdoms of the world in a moment of time.

And the devil said unto him, All this power will I give thee, and the glory of them: for that is delivered unto me; and to whomsoever I will I give it.

If thou therefore wilt worship me, all shall be thine.

And Jesus answered and said unto him, Get thee behind me, Satan: for it is written, Thou shalt worship the Lord thy God, and him only shalt thou serve. (Luke 4:1–8.)

"Get Behind Me, Satan"

Sister Anna Widtsoe was first introduced to the restored gospel by a cobbler who put missionary tracts in her children's shoes which he had repaired. She was at first incensed that a businessman would do such a thing, but as they spoke she became interested and eventually converted. Her son, John Widtsoe, would later become the president of the University of Utah and a member of the Council of the Twelve Apostles. He shared this story about his mother's determination to keep the commandments:

> She had not been taught the Word of Wisdom, except as it had been mentioned casually in gospel conversations. Now, she began to understand its real meaning and purpose and the necessity of obeying it since it was the desire of the Father that His children should heed it. Following the custom of most of her country people she had drunk coffee from her childhood and was an occasional user of tea. Alcoholic beverages she did not use. She set about to give up the use of tea and coffee but found it difficult. When she sewed every night far beyond midnight, the cup of coffee seemed to freshen her, she thought. After a two months' struggle, she came home one day, having given serious consideration to the Word of Wisdom problem. Her mind was made up. She stood in the middle of the room and said aloud, "Never again. Get behind me, Satan!" and, walking briskly to her cupboard, took out the packages of coffee and tea and threw them on the fire. From that day she never used tea or coffee. (John A. Widtsoe, *In the Gospel Net* [Salt Lake City: Bookcraft, 1966], p. 87.)

"Restored Whole"

Luke 6:6–10

"And it came to pass also on another sabbath, that he entered into the synagogue and taught: and there was a man whose right hand was withered.

"And the scribes and Pharisees watched him, whether he would heal on the sabbath day; that they might find an accusation against him.

"But he knew their thoughts, and said to the man which had the withered hand, Rise up, and stand forth in the midst. And he arose and stood forth.

"Then said Jesus unto them, I will ask you one thing; Is it lawful on the sabbath days to do good, or to do evil? to save life, or to destroy it?

"And looking round about upon them all, he said unto the man, Stretch forth thy hand. And he did so: and his hand was restored whole as the other." (Luke 6:6–10.)

Her Crippled Arm Was as Good as the Other One

In the spring of 1831 a Methodist preacher named Ezra Booth brought a party to Kirtland, which included a well-to-do farmer named John Johnson and his wife, Elsa, from Hiram, Ohio. Elsa's arm was partially paralyzed from rheumatism, and she could not raise it above her head. As they talked with the Prophet, one of the visitors asked if there was anyone on earth who had the power to cure Elsa's lame arm. When the conversation turned to another subject, Joseph went up to Mrs. Johnson, took her by the hand, and with calm assurance said, "Woman, in the name of the Lord Jesus Christ I command thee to be whole." As Joseph went from the room, leaving everyone astonished and speechless, she raised her arm. The next day she hung out her first wash in over six years without any pain. Ezra Booth and some members of the Johnson family joined the Church as a result of the healing. The miracle also attracted wide acclaim throughout northern Ohio. (*Church History in the Fulness of Times* [Salt Lake City: The Church of Jesus Christ of Latter-day Saints, 1989], pp. 93–94.)

Arise, Come Forth!

Luke 7:11–16; John 11:1–45

And it came to pass the day after, that he went into a city called Nain; and many of his disciples went with him, and much people.

Now when he came nigh to the gate of the city, behold, there was a dead man carried out, the only son of his mother, and she was a widow: and much people of the city was with her.

And when the Lord saw her, he had compassion on her, and said unto her, Weep not.

And he came and touched the bier: and they that bare him stood still. And he said, Young man, I say unto thee, Arise.

And he that was dead sat up, and began to speak. And he delivered him to his mother.

And there came a fear on all: and they glorified God, saying, That a great prophet is risen up among us; and, That God hath visited his people. (Luke 7:11–16.)

Now a certain man was sick, named Lazarus, of Bethany, the town of Mary and her sister Martha.

(It was that Mary which anointed the Lord with ointment, and wiped his feet with her hair, whose brother Lazarus was sick.)

Therefore his sisters sent unto him, saying, Lord, behold, he whom thou lovest is sick.

When Jesus heard that, he said, This sickness is not unto death, but for the glory of God, that the Son of God might be glorified thereby.

Now Jesus loved Martha, and her sister, and Lazarus.

When he had heard therefore that he was sick, he abode two days still in the same place where he was.

Then after that saith he to his disciples, Let us go into Judaea again.

His disciples say unto him, Master, the Jews of late sought to stone thee; and goest thou thither again?

Jesus answered, Are there not twelve hours in the day? If any man walk in the day, he stumbleth not, because he seeth the light of this world.

But if a man walk in the night, he stumbleth, because there is no light in him.

These things said he: and after that he saith unto them, Our friend Lazarus sleepeth; but I go, that I may awake him out of sleep.

Then said his disciples, Lord, if he sleep, he shall do well.

Howbeit Jesus spake of his death: but they thought that he had spoken of taking of rest in sleep.

Then said Jesus unto them plainly, Lazarus is dead.

And I am glad for your sakes that I was not there, to the intent ye may believe; nevertheless let us go unto him.

Then said Thomas, which is called Didymus, unto his fellow disciples, Let us also go, that we may die with him.

Then when Jesus came, he found that he had lain in the grave four days already.

Now Bethany was nigh unto Jerusalem, about fifteen furlongs off:

And many of the Jews came to Martha and Mary, to comfort them concerning their brother.

Then Martha, as soon as she heard that Jesus was coming, went and met him: but Mary sat still in the house.

Then said Martha unto Jesus, Lord, if thou hadst been here, my brother had not died.

But I know, that even now, whatsoever thou wilt ask of God, God will give it thee.

Jesus saith unto her, Thy brother shall rise again.

Martha saith unto him, I know that he shall rise again in the resurrection at the last day.

Jesus said unto her, I am the resurrection, and the life: he that believeth in me, though he were dead, yet shall he live:

And whosoever liveth and believeth in me shall never die. Believest thou this?

She saith unto him, Yea, Lord: I believe that thou art the Christ, the Son of God, which should come into the world.

And when she had so said, she went her way, and called Mary her sister secretly, saying, The Master is come, and calleth for thee.

As soon as she heard that, she arose quickly, and came unto him.

Now Jesus was not yet come into the town, but was in that place where Martha met him.

The Jews then which were with her in the house, and comforted her, when they saw Mary, that she rose up hastily and went out, followed her, saying, She goeth unto the grave to weep there.

Then when Mary was come where Jesus was, and saw him, she fell down at his feet, saying unto him, Lord, if thou hadst been here, my brother had not died.

When Jesus therefore saw her weeping, and the Jews also weeping which came with her, he groaned in the spirit, and was troubled,

And said, Where have ye laid him? They said unto him, Lord, come and see.

Jesus wept.

Then said the Jews, Behold how he loved him!

And some of them said, Could not this man, which opened the eyes of the blind, have caused that even this man should not have died?

Jesus therefore again groaning in himself cometh to the grave. It was a cave, and a stone lay upon it.

Jesus said, Take ye away the stone. Martha, the sister of him that was dead, saith unto him, Lord, by this time he stinketh: for he hath been dead four days.

Jesus saith unto her, Said I not unto thee, that, if thou wouldest believe, thou shouldest see the glory of God?

Then they took away the stone from the place where the dead was laid. And Jesus lifted up his eyes, and said, Father, I thank thee that thou hast heard me.

And I knew that thou hearest me always: but because of

the people which stand by I said it, that they may believe that thou hast sent me.

And when he thus had spoken, he cried with a loud voice, Lazarus, come forth.

And he that was dead came forth, bound hand and foot with graveclothes: and his face was bound about with a napkin. Jesus saith unto them, Loose him, and let him go.

Then many of the Jews which came to Mary, and had seen the things which Jesus did, believed on him. (John 11:1–45.)

"I Never Felt Better in My Life"

About the month of August, 1856, William D. Huntington and I [Levi Curtis] went into Hobble Creek Canyon to get a log suitable for making drums. After we . . . started for home, . . . our conversation naturally turned upon the . . . experiences of the past, when the life and labors of the Prophet Joseph were touched upon. This subject aroused into more than usual earnestness the mind and conversation of my associate.

He said that in Nauvoo he lived in the family of and worked for Joseph Smith at the time the Prophet had such a wonderful time with the sick. . . . He said he had been sick some weeks and kept getting weaker, until he became so helpless that he could not move. Finally he got so low he could not speak, but had perfect consciousness of all that was passing in the room. He saw friends come to the bedside, look at him a moment and commence weeping, then turn away.

He further stated that he presently felt easy, and . . . found that he was in the upper part of the room near the ceiling, and could see the body he had occupied lying on the bed, with weeping friends standing around.

About this time he saw Joseph Smith and two other brethren come into the room. Joseph turned to his wife Emma and asked her to get him a dish of clean water. This she did; and the Prophet with the two brethren . . . washed their hands and carefully wiped them. Then they stepped to the bed and laid their hands upon the head of his body, which at that time looked loathsome to him, and as the three stretched out their hands to place them upon the head, he by some means became aware that he must go back into that body, and started to do so. The process of getting in he could not remember; but when Joseph said "amen," he heard and could see and feel with his body. The feeling for a moment was most excruciating, as though his body was pierced in every part with some sharp instruments.

As soon as the brethren had taken their hands from his head he raised up in bed, sitting erect, and in another moment turned his legs off the bed.

At this juncture Joseph asked him if he had not better be careful, for he was very weak. He replied, "I never felt better in my life," almost immediately adding, "I want my pants."

His pants were found and given to him, which he drew on, Joseph assisting him, although he thought he needed no help. Then he signified his intention to sit in a chair at or near the fireplace. Joseph took hold of his arm to help him along safely, but William declared his ability to walk alone, notwithstanding which, the help continued.

Astonishment had taken the place of weeping throughout the room. Every looker-on was ready to weep for joy; but none were able or felt inclined to talk.

Presently William said he wanted something to eat. Joseph asked him what he would like, and he replied that he wanted a dish of bread and milk.

Emma immediately brought what he called for, . . . every hand was anxious to supply the wants of a man who, a few moments before was dead, really and truly dead! Brother Huntington ate the bowl of bread and milk with as good a relish as any he ever ate.

In a short time all felt more familiar, and conversation upon the scene that transpired followed. William related his experiences, and the friends theirs.

Joseph listened to the conversation and in his turn remarked that they had just witnessed as great a miracle as Jesus did while on the earth. They had seen the dead brought to life.

At the close of his narrative to me, William Huntington remarked:

"Now I have told you the truth, and here I am a live man, sitting by the side of you on this log, and I testify that Joseph Smith was a prophet of God." (*Juvenile Instructor,* June 1892, pp. 385–86.)

Building the Kingdom

Luke 7:37–38

"And, behold, a woman in the city, which was a sinner, when she knew that Jesus sat at meat in the Pharisee's house, brought an alabaster box of ointment,

"And stood at his feet behind him weeping, and began to wash his feet with tears, and did wipe them with the hairs of her head, and kissed his feet, and anointed them with the ointment." (Luke 7:37–38.)

"Here Is All I Have"

Alan K. Parrish and Susan Easton Black shared the following story about an early member of the Church, Lydia Goldthwaite, who was willing to sacrifice all she had for the Lord's anointed.

Lydia, recently separated from her husband, had just arrived in Kirtland when she was approached by Vincent Knight, who exclaimed:

"Sister, the Prophet is in bondage and has been brought into distress by the persecutions of the wicked, and if you have any means to give, it will be a benefit to him."

"Oh yes, sir," she replied, "here is all I have. I only wish it was more," emptying her purse, containing perhaps fifty dollars, in his hand as she spoke.

He looked at it and counted it and fervently exclaimed: "Thank God, this will release and set the Prophet free!"

The young girl was without means now, even to procure a meal or a night's lodging. Still that sweet spirit that rested upon her whispered "all will be well."

As evening drew on, Vincent Knight returned and brought the welcome news that Joseph was at liberty, and Lydia's joy to think that she had been the humble means of helping the Prophet was unbounded. (As quoted in *The New Testament and the Latter-day Saints* [Orem, Utah: Randall Book Company, 1987], p. 55.)

Virtue Went
Out from Him

Luke 8:43–48

"And a woman having an issue of blood twelve years, which had spent all her living upon physicians, neither could be healed of any,

"Came behind him, and touched the border of his garment: and immediately her issue of blood stanched [ceased].

"And Jesus said, Who touched me? When all denied, Peter and they that were with him said, Master, the multitude throng thee and press thee, and sayest thou, Who touched me?

"And Jesus said, Somebody hath touched me: for I perceive that virtue is gone out of me.

"And when the woman saw that she was not hid, she came trembling, and falling down before him, she declared unto him before all the people for what cause she had touched him, and how she was healed immediately.

"And he said unto her, Daughter, be of good comfort: thy faith hath made thee whole; go in peace." (Luke 8:43–48.)

"Virtue Went Out of Me into the Children"

Joseph Smith, under the date of 14 March 1843, wrote in his journal:

Elder Jedediah M. Grant enquired of me the cause of my turning pale and losing strength last night while blessing children. I told him that I saw that Lucifer would exert his influence to destroy the children that I was blessing, and I strove with all the faith and spirit that I had to seal upon them a blessing that would secure their lives upon the earth; and so much virtue went out of me into the children, that I became weak, from which I have not yet recovered; and I referred to the case of the woman touching the hem of the garment of Jesus. . . . The virtue referred to is the spirit of life; and a man who exercises great faith in administering to the sick, blessing little children, or confirming, is liable to become weakened. (*Teachings of the Prophet Joseph Smith* [Salt Lake City: Deseret Book Co., 1976], pp. 280–81.)

Elder Bruce R. McConkie has written that "giving blessings and performing priesthood ordinances is often the most physically taxing labor which the Lord's true ministers ever perform. There is nothing perfunctory or casual about the performance of these holy ordinances; great physical exertion and intense mental concentration are part of the struggle to get that spirit of revelation so essential in an inspired blessing or other performance." (*Doctrinal New Testament Commentary*, vol. 1 [Salt Lake City: Bookcraft, 1973], p. 319.)

The Good Samaritan

Luke 10:25–37

And, behold, a certain lawyer stood up, and tempted him, saying, Master, what shall I do to inherit eternal life?

He said unto him, What is written in the law? how readest thou?

And he answering said, Thou shalt love the Lord thy God with all thy heart, and with all thy soul, and with all thy strength, and with all thy mind; and thy neighbour as thyself.

And he said unto him, Thou hast answered right: this do, and thou shalt live.

But he, willing to justify himself, said unto Jesus, And who is my neighbour?

And Jesus answering said, A certain man went down from Jerusalem to Jericho, and fell among thieves, which stripped him of his raiment, and wounded him, and departed, leaving him half dead.

And by chance there came down a certain priest that way: and when he saw him, he passed by on the other side.

And likewise a Levite, when he was at the place, came and looked on him, and passed by on the other side.

But a certain Samaritan, as he journeyed, came where he was: and when he saw him, he had compassion on him,

And went to him, and bound up his wounds, pouring in oil and wine, and set him on his own beast, and brought him to an inn, and took care of him.

And on the morrow when he departed, he took out two pence, and gave them to the host, and said unto him, Take care of him; and whatsoever thou spendest more, when I come again, I will repay thee.

Which now of these three, thinkest thou, was neighbour unto him that fell among the thieves?

And he said, He that shewed mercy on him. Then said Jesus unto him, Go, and do thou likewise. (Luke 10:25–37.)

Samaritan in Mexico

It was a late winter night when my friend Dick [Richard A.] Lambert phoned. He and his wife, Mary, were going to Mexico City. They were going to take along their daughter and four sons, all of them under 13. We had made the drive the previous year.

As spring's green began to streak our valley, the Lamberts rolled south toward Old Mexico. The next two weeks were a wonderland of scenery and sights. They saw the plodding burros everywhere in Mexico, the Mexican men in broad-brimmed straw hats and the women with their colorful shawls. They saw oxen pulling wooden plows in the fields, and they beheld the pyramids and Mexico City's modern skyscrapers, sleek with sweeping walls of concrete, metal, and glass. For days, their eyes had a feast.

Then the two-tone Lambert sedan, of Texas tan and cream, turned northward toward home. The children were still laughing. They had souvenirs—beautiful leather belts and purses and pocketbooks. They pushed toward Lagos de Moreno, about 300 miles north of Mexico City. This was in the high, rolling prairie country of central Mexico. A warm sun smiled on the travelers. Mary was now at the wheel.

The car approached a road junction. The signs were in Spanish. Mary's eyes studied the signs a second too long. The big car roared off the highway, spun crazily and then rolled over three times.

The car stopped upright, a battered heap. Dick was under it, unconscious with a broken nose and foot, five broken teeth, and a generally cut and beaten body. Mary, too, had been hurled from the car, but escaped with minor cuts and bruises. The youngest child, 5-year-old Chris, had also been thrown from the car. He, too, was unconscious. The four other children were still in the car. They had no serious hurts.

Almost immediately after the accident, a busload of Mexicans stopped. Some tried to give assistance. With the help of a Mexican motorist, an ambulance and a truck, the family was taken to Lagos for treatment at the Red Cross station.

Only the wreck that had been a car remained.

Then there drove past the accident scene a middle-aged Mexican couple in a dark sedan. He was a short, rather plump man with graying black hair and keen, brown eyes. He wore a straw business hat, a short-sleeved sport shirt and light trousers. His name was Edmundo Martinez G. He was owner of a small ice cream plant in Guadalajara, Mexico's second largest city, about 150 miles west of the accident scene. He was homeward bound from Mexico City.

Edmundo Martinez pressed his brake. Someone had been seriously injured, if not killed, in this accident. His eyes caught the American license plate. That told him another tragic story. He knew that the owner of the car, if he survived, would have trouble—much trouble—with customs and the language. The laws are strict about tourists entering the country with an automobile and leaving without one.

Edmundo Martinez could speak English. He had worked for Henry Ford in Detroit. He had pressing matters at home in Guadalajara. It was only a few days before the Holy Week, one of the big ice cream seasons of the year in Mexico.

But Edmundo Martinez at the junction took the road to the right, to Lagos, instead of the one to the left, to his home.

He found the Lamberts at the Red Cross station. He gathered the children into his car and took them to the hotel. Little Chris, still unconscious, was with them. The children's new friend rented a room for them and left his wife, who did not speak English, with them. He returned to the hospital, where Dick Lambert's cuts were stitched. Then he drove Dick and Mary to the hotel. He provided the family with dinner. Then he said, "I'm staying in the room right next to yours. Call me if you need me."

Next day, Mr. Martinez drove 33 miles to Leon, and there

paid the Lamberts' fine—280 pesos (about $32). He boxed up all their belongings and shipped them to Guadalajara. That night he drove all the Lamberts to Guadalajara. Riding in the front seat with him and Mrs. Martinez was Kent, the Lambert's six-year-old who was almost dark enough to be a Mexican. The children sang Latter-day Saint Sunday School hymns as they rode—that is, all the children but little Chris. He was still unconscious.

Mr. Martinez arranged lodgings for the American family at a Guadalajara hotel. The next morning he took four of them to the hospital for further medical attention. Guadalajara's beautiful blue-lavender jacaranda tree blooms helped brighten that morning. So did the return to consciousness of little Chris.

The Lamberts were five days in Guadalajara. There was surgery for Chris and a plaster cast for Dick. Edmundo Martinez was always there when he was needed—in person or on the phone. Daily he brought ice cream for the family. He took their clothes to the cleaners, and he spent a good part of two days clearing red tape with customs.

On the Lamberts' last night before enplaning from Mexico, their friend visited them at the hotel. He handed them 48 American dollars and 200 Mexican pesos. "I don't want you to have any trouble in getting home," he said. Meanwhile, he had troubles of his own, with the freezing equipment at the plant.

Mary was the last Lambert to say good-by to Edmundo Martinez. She accompanied him to the hotel elevator. Tears were not far from her bright blue eyes. Her clear, rich voice fought with emotion. She is a pretty, black-haired young woman. "Mr. Martinez," she began, "we want to make it right with you after we return home. We can never fully repay you. But what do we owe you in expense?"

"You don't owe me anything," the Mexican replied. He still wore a short-sleeved sport shirt. "Just remember me in your prayers."

With that, he was gone.

The day Dick Lambert arrived home, he mailed a check to his Mexican friend.

Later Edmundo Martinez wrote to the Lamberts. He was

still getting papers signed and red tape cleared in connection with their insurance and other matters. "My wife joins me in sending love to all the family," he concluded. "Halo, Kenny [Kent]. Don't forget your friend."

How could anyone forget a friend like Edmundo Martinez G.? (Wendell J. Ashton, "Samaritan in Mexico," *Instructor*, February 1955, back cover.)

The Desire to Hear the Word of God

Luke 10:38–39

"Now it came to pass, as they went, that he entered into a certain village: and a certain woman named Martha received him into her house.

"And she had a sister called Mary, which also sat at Jesus' feet, and heard his word." (Luke 10:38–39.)

Mary Elizabeth Rollins and the Book of Mormon

The desire to hear the word of God is one of the distinguishing characteristics of the elect. "And he that will hear my voice shall be my sheep" (Mosiah 26:21). Mary Elizabeth Rollins, a young girl in Kirtland, learned that Brother Isaac Morley had the only copy of the Book of Mormon in the community. She later wrote, "I went to his house . . . and asked to see the Book; Brother Morley put it in my hand, as I looked at it, I felt such a desire to read it, that I could not refrain from asking him to let me take it home and read it."

True to her word, she returned it early the next morning. "When I handed him the book, he remarked, 'I guess you did not read much in it.' I showed him how far [my family and I] had read. He was surprised, and said, 'I don't believe you can tell me one word of it.' I then repeated the first verse, also the outlines of the history of Nephi. He gazed at me in surprise, and said, 'child, take this book home and finish it, I can wait.'"

About the time Mary finished reading the book, Joseph Smith and Emma moved to Kirtland. The Prophet, while visiting the Rollins' home, noticed the Book of Mormon and recognized it as the copy he had given to Brother Morley. When he learned about Mary's earnest desire to read it, he sent for her. "When he saw me he looked at me so earnestly, I felt almost afraid. After a moment or two he came and put his hands on my head and gave me a great blessing, the first I ever received, and made me a present of the book, and said he would give Brother Morley another." ("Mary Elizabeth Rollins Lightner," *Utah Genealogical and Historical Magazine*, July 1926, pp. 193–205, 250–60.)

The Faith and Desire
to Be Healed

Luke 13:11–13

"And, behold, there was a woman which had a spirit of infirmity eighteen years, and was bowed together, and could in no wise lift up herself.

"And when Jesus saw her, he called her to him, and said unto her, Woman, thou art loosed from thine infirmity.

"And he laid his hands on her: and immediately she was made straight, and glorified God." (Luke 13:11–13.)

Immediately Loosed from Infirmity

Isabella Park, a sixty-two-year-old member of Captain McArthur's second handcart company, was a recipient of the Lord's healing blessing by being loosed from her infirmity. Wilford Woodruff reported an accident that Isabella had on the journey west:

> Old Sister Isabella Park ran in before the wagon to see how her [sick] companion was. The driver, not seeing her, hallooed at his team and they being quick to mind, Sister Park could not get out of the way, and the fore wheel struck her and threw her down and passed over both her hips. Brother Leonard grabbed hold of her to pull her out of the way, before the hind wheel could catch her. He only got her

out part way and the hind wheels passed over her ankles. We all thought that she would be all mashed to pieces, but to the joy of us all, there was not a bone broken, although the wagon had something like two tons burden on it, a load for 4 yoke of oxen. We went right to work [giving a priesthood blessing] and applied the same medicine to her that we did to the sister who was bitten by the rattlesnake, and although quite sore for a few days, Sister Park got better, so that she was on the tramp before we got into this Valley. (As quoted in LeRoy R. and Ann W. Hafen, *Handcarts to Zion* [Glendale, California: Arthur H. Clark Co., 1960], pp. 216–17.)

A Lost Piece of Silver

Luke 15:8–10

"Either what woman having ten pieces of silver, if she lose one piece, doth not light a candle, and sweep the house, and seek diligently till she find it?

"And when she hath found it, she calleth her friends and her neighbours together, saying, Rejoice with me; for I have found the piece which I had lost.

"Likewise, I say unto you, there is joy in the presence of the angels of God over one sinner that repenteth." (Luke 15:8–10.)

Our "Lost Coin"

Though it was several years ago, I can still recall the panic I felt that day as I searched my house for the misplaced envelope containing six hundred dollars. Frantically, I dumped drawers and searched the desk where I usually put important papers.

As the mother of three young children and the wife of a school teacher, I knew how much we needed that money. I knew how far off our next monthly payday was.

I prayed, and so did our whole family. All our family prayers centered around pleas for help in locating that envelope, yet we received no answer. I wondered how I could have been so irresponsible. We needed that money in order to pay bills and buy food. Time passed, and each day frustration and fear took a greater hold on my spirit and my faith. The lost money occupied all my thoughts.

A few weeks later on Sunday, I remembered that a visiting teaching message meeting would take place before Relief Society. I decided I would be better off at church than at home worrying about the money, and I managed to get all three children into the nursery and slip into my seat just as the teacher began her lesson. She was reading the parable of the lost piece of silver from the Bible. (See Luke 15:8–10.)

Suddenly it was no longer just a parable, but an instant replay of the past three weeks at our house, where nothing had been left unturned and where I had spent long hours trying to reconstruct my actions.

Then the Spirit whispered that while the Savior sought after the lost soul, I had been seeking the piece of silver. I realized that if I used the same energy to find the sisters I was assigned to visit that I had spent trying to find our six hundred dollars, I could truly magnify my visiting teaching calling.

Tears ran down my cheeks as the lesson hit home, and I knew something good would still come of the experience. The panic and the self-recrimination were gone, and I knew through the peaceful reassurance of the Spirit that somehow all would be well.

For the first time in weeks I felt really happy again. The children sensed a difference. When we got home, we all knelt together, and four-year-old Spencer prayed once more that we would find our money.

Then we got up, and with no conscious thought, went to our seldom-used front entry closet. There on the top shelf was a book with the envelope of money sticking out of it. Prayers had been answered, a lesson taught, and the money recovered.

Today, our two older children bear testimony to the younger ones that Heavenly Father does answer our prayers, and I understand in a much more personal way that the worth of souls is great in the sight of God. (Paula Schulthess Anderson, "Our 'Lost Coin,'" *Ensign*, September 1987, pp. 53–54.)

The Prodigal Son

Luke 15:11–32

And he said, A certain man had two sons:

And the younger of them said to his father, Father, give me the portion of goods that falleth to me. And he divided unto them his living.

And not many days after the younger son gathered all together, and took his journey into a far country, and there wasted his substance with riotous living.

And when he had spent all, there arose a mighty famine in that land; and he began to be in want.

And he went and joined himself to a citizen of that country; and he sent him into his fields to feed swine.

And he would fain have filled his belly with the husks that the swine did eat: and no man gave unto him.

And when he came to himself, he said, How many hired servants of my father's have bread enough and to spare, and I perish with hunger!

I will arise and go to my father, and will say unto him, Father, I have sinned against heaven, and before thee,

And am no more worthy to be called thy son: make me as one of thy hired servants.

And he arose, and came to his father. But when he was yet a great way off, his father saw him, and had compassion, and ran, and fell on his neck, and kissed him.

And the son said unto him, Father, I have sinned against heaven, and in thy sight, and am no more worthy to be called thy son.

But the father said to his servants, Bring forth the best robe, and put it on him; and put a ring on his hand, and shoes on his feet:

And bring hither the fatted calf, and kill it; and let us eat, and be merry:

For this my son was dead, and is alive again; he was lost, and is found. And they began to be merry.

Now his elder son was in the field: and as he came and drew nigh to the house, he heard musick and dancing.

And he called one of the servants, and asked what these things meant.

And he said unto him, Thy brother is come; and thy father hath killed the fatted calf, because he hath received him safe and sound.

And he was angry, and would not go in: therefore came his father out, and intreated him.

And he answering said to his father, Lo, these many years do I serve thee, neither transgressed I at any time thy commandment: and yet thou never gavest me a kid, that I might make merry with my friends:

But as soon as this thy son was come, which hath devoured thy living with harlots, thou hast killed for him the fatted calf.

And he said unto him, Son, thou art ever with me, and all that I have is thine.

It was meet that we should make merry, and be glad: for this thy brother was dead, and is alive again; and was lost, and is found. (Luke 15:11–32.)

The Return of the Prodigal

Until I was 17 years of age, I stayed close to the Church, attending all my meetings and carrying out my priesthood responsibilities. It did not occur to me to do otherwise. I loved the Church and its programs.

At 17, however, I began to "flex my teenage muscles," rebelling against family direction and demanding my "free agency." One of my best friends was of another faith, and I fell into the trap of trying some of the things he offered—

alcohol, tobacco. I dated non-LDS girls and soon fell in love with a wonderful young lady. Her parents invited me to their summer cabin on many weekends, and this, of course, kept me from church activity.

Then World War II came along, and when my bishop asked me if I wanted to go on a mission, I said I would rather join the military and serve my country. I still believe serving one's country is important, but I know now that I would have been wiser to serve a mission for my Heavenly Father first.

Also, about this time, I began finding out that some Church members whom I admired greatly were not observing all the standards of the Church. I let myself become their judge, and to me they were hypocrites. I covenanted with myself that if I ever failed to live our standards, rather than be a hypocrite by teaching one thing and doing another, I would stay away from the Church. This was another serious error, for this is just what I did and just what the adversary wanted.

Four years as a Navy pilot and 15 years of traveling in the sales profession made it easy for me to remain inactive, yet all during these years I believed the truths that were deeply implanted in my soul. When I was 38, my youngest brother, Tom, moved in with us for six weeks. Each Sunday morning he went alone to his priesthood and other meetings, and my conscience began to prick me. I wasn't happy, I knew something was wrong, and this feeling kept coming back with greater frequency. In the past I had been able to give up smoking whenever I wanted, but now I found I could not. I would visit Tom in his office and find myself striking out at the Church in criticism, and afterwards, although I would never tell him so, I felt guilty.

I was building up to my hour of crisis, and it came one night after a cocktail party and dance at the country club. I retired to my bed late but could not sleep, almost unheard of for me. Finally I arose so as not to disturb my lovely wife, and for the first time in my life I paced the floor, finally realizing I had to change.

I had never been able to show emotion through tears and humility, but the next thing I remember I was on my knees pleading with my Heavenly Father for help for the first time in 19 years. As I prayed, an overwhelming feeling of love and compassion and happiness filled my being, and the Holy Ghost encompassed me with such power that I sobbed convulsively for a considerable time. When I arose, I felt good. Gratitude and thankfulness filled my heart. Never in my life had I known such a feeling of warmth, and an inner burning filled my entire being with such intensity that I thought I was going to be consumed.

I went to our bedroom and awakened my wife. I was still crying, and she asked me what was wrong. I told her of my desire to change my life and encompass the gospel of Jesus Christ, and she told me instantly that she would support me. From that moment I have never had a desire for a cigarette, a drink of any type, or a cup of coffee.

The Lord began blessing me, and he has never stopped to this day. Within a year it was my privilege to baptize my children and, soon afterward, my wife. A year later we went to the Logan Temple to be married for eternity and to have our children sealed to us.

I testify that the Lord is pleased when his lost sheep come home. He shows his love and kindness to all of us when we repent of our sins and keep his commandments. (Lewis W. Cottle, "Return of the Prodigal," *Ensign*, March 1974, pp. 43–44.)

"He That Is Greatest Among You"

Luke 22:14–15, 24–27

"And when the hour was come, he sat down, and the twelve apostles with him.

"And he said unto them, With desire I have desired to eat this passover with you before I suffer . . .

"And there was also a strife among them, which of them should be accounted the greatest.

"And he said unto them, The kings of the Gentiles exercise lordship over them; and they that exercise authority upon them are called benefactors.

"But ye shall not be so: but he that is greatest among you, let him be as the younger; and he that is chief, as he that doth serve.

"For whether is greater, he that sitteth at meat, or he that serveth? is not he that sitteth at meat? but I am among you as he that serveth." (Luke 22:14–15, 24–27.)

The Helpful Stranger

A young mother on an overnight flight with a two-year-old daughter was stranded by bad weather in the Chicago airport without food or clean clothing for the child and without money. She was two months pregnant and threatened with miscarriage, so she was under doctor's instructions not to carry the child unless it was essential. Hour after hour she stood in one line after another, trying to get a flight to Michigan. The terminal was noisy, full of tired, frustrated, grumpy passengers, and she heard critical references to her crying child and to her sliding her child along the floor with her foot as the line moved forward. No one offered to help with the soaked, hungry, exhausted child. Then, the woman later reported, "someone came towards us and with a kindly smile said, 'Is there something I could do to help you?' With a grateful sigh I accepted his offer. He lifted my sobbing little daughter from the cold floor and lovingly held her to him while he patted her gently on the back. He asked if she could chew a piece of gum. When she was settled down, he carried her with him and said something kindly to the others in the line ahead of me, about how I needed their help. They seemed to agree and then he went up to the ticket counter [at the front of the line] and made arrangements with the clerk for me to be put on a flight leaving shortly. He walked with us to a bench, where we chatted a moment, until he was assured that I would be fine. He went on his way. About a week later I saw a picture of Apostle Spencer W. Kimball and recognized him as the stranger in the airport." (Edward L. Kimball and Andrew E. Kimball, Jr., *Spencer W. Kimball* [Salt Lake City: Bookcraft, 1977, p. 334.)

Unjust Judges
and False Accusations

Luke 22:63–71; 23:1–7

And the men that held Jesus mocked him, and smote him.

And when they had blindfolded him, they struck him on the face, and asked him, saying, Prophesy, who is it that smote thee?

And many other things blasphemously spake they against him.

And as soon as it was day, the elders of the people and the chief priests and the scribes came together, and led him into their council, saying,

Art thou the Christ? tell us. And he said unto them, If I tell you, ye will not believe:

And if I also ask you, ye will not answer me, nor let me go.

Hereafter shall the Son of man sit on the right hand of the power of God.

Then said they all, Art thou then the Son of God? And he said unto them, Ye say that I am.

And they said, What need we any further witness? for we ourselves have heard of his own mouth.

And the whole multitude of them arose, and led him unto Pilate.

And they began to accuse him, saying, We found this fellow perverting the nation, and forbidding to give tribute to Caesar, saying that he himself is Christ a King.

And Pilate asked him, saying, Art thou the King of the Jews? And he answered him and said, Thou sayest it.

Then said Pilate to the chief priests and to the people, I find no fault in this man.

And they were the more fierce, saying, He stirreth up the people, teaching throughout all Jewry, beginning from Galilee to this place.

When Pilate heard of Galilee, he asked whether the man were a Galilaean.

And as soon as he knew that he belonged unto Herod's jurisdiction, he sent him to Herod, who himself also was at Jerusalem at that time. (Luke 22:63–71; 23:1–7.)

Arrested on Frivilous Charges at the House of Simeon Carter

Parley P. Pratt wrote:

We had stopped for the night at the house of Simeon Carter, by whom we were kindly received, and were in the act of reading to him and explaining the Book of Mormon, when there came a knock at the door, and an officer entered with a warrant from a magistrate by the name of Byington, to arrest me on a very frivolous charge. I dropped the Book of Mormon in Carter's house, and went with him some two miles, in a dark, muddy road; one of the brethren accompanied me. We arrived at the place of trial late in the evening; found false witnesses in attendance, and a Judge who boasted of his intention to thrust us into prison, for the purpose of testing the powers of our apostleship, as he called it; although I was only an Elder in the Church. The Judge boasting thus, and the witnesses being entirely false in their testimony, I concluded to make no defense, but to treat the whole matter with contempt.

I was soon ordered to prison, or to pay a sum of money which I had not in the world. It was now a late hour, and I was still retained in court, tantalized, abused and urged to settle the matter, to all of which I made no reply for some time. This greatly exhausted their patience. It was near midnight. I now called on brother Petersen to sing a hymn in the court. We sung, "O how happy are they." This exasperated them still more, and they pressed us greatly to settle the business, by paying the money.

I then observed as follows: "May it please the court, I have one proposal to make for a final settlement of the things that seem to trouble you. It is this: if the witnesses who have given testimony in the case will repent of their false swearing, and the magistrate of his unjust and wicked judgment and of his persecution, blackguardism and abuse, and all kneel down together, we will pray for you, that God might forgive you in these matters."

"My big bull dog pray for me," says that Judge.

"The devil help us," exclaimed another.

They now urged me for some time to pay the money; but got no further answer.

The court adjourned, and I was conducted to a public house over the way, and locked in till morning; the prison being some miles distant.

In the morning the officer appeared and took me to breakfast; this over, we sat waiting in the inn for all things to be ready to conduct me to prison. In the meantime my fellow travellers came past on their journey, and called to see me. I told them in an undertone to pursue their journey and leave me to manage my own affairs, promising to overtake them soon. They did so.

After sitting awhile by the fire in charge of the officer, I requested to step out. I walked out into the public square accompanied by him. Said I, "Mr. Peabody, are you good at a race?" "No," said he, "but my big bull dog is, and he has been trained to assist me in my office these several years; he will take any man down at my bidding." "Well, Mr. Peabody, you compelled me to go a mile, I have gone with you two miles. You have given me an opportunity to preach, sing, and have also entertained me with lodging and breakfast. I must now go on my journey; if you are good at a race you can accompany me. I thank you for all your kindness—good day, sir."

I then started on my journey, while he stood amazed and not able to step one foot before the other. Seeing this, I halted, turned to him and again invited him to a race. He still stood amazed. I then renewed my exertions, and soon increased my speed to something like that of a deer. He did not awake from his astonishment sufficiently to start in pursuit till I had gained, perhaps, two hundred yards. I had already leaped a fence, and was making my way through a field to the forest on the right of the road. He now came hallooing after me, and shouting to his dog to seize me. The dog, being one of the largest I ever saw, came close on my footsteps with all his fury; the officer behind still in pursuit, clapping his hands and hallooing, "stu-boy, stu-boy—take him—watch—lay hold of him, I say—down with him," and pointing his finger in the direction I was running. The dog was fast overtaking me, and in the act of leaping upon me, when, quick as lightning, the thought struck me, to assist the officer, in sending the dog with all fury to the forest a little distance before me. I pointed my finger in that direction, clapped my hands, and shouted in imitation of the officer. The dog hastened past me with redoubled speed towards the forest; being urged by the officer and myself, and both of us running in the same direction.

Gaining the forest, I soon lost sight of the officer and dog, and have not seen them since. I took a back course, crossed the road, took round into the wilderness, on the left, and made the road again in time to cross a bridge over Vermilion River, where I was hailed by half a dozen men, who had been anxiously waiting our arrival to that part of the country, and who urged me very earnestly to stop and preach. I told them that I could not then do it, for an officer was on my track. I passed on six miles further, through mud and rain, and overtook the brethren, and preached the same evening to a crowded audience, among whom we were well entertained.

The Book of Mormon, which I dropped at the house of Simeon Carter, when taken by the officer, was by these circumstances left with him. He read it with attention. It wrought deeply upon his mind, and he went fifty miles to the church we had left in Kirtland, and was there baptized and ordained an Elder. He then returned to his home and commenced to preach and baptize. A church of about sixty members was soon organized in the place where I had played such a trick of deception on the dog. (*Autobiography of Parley P. Pratt*, reprint ed. [Salt Lake City: Deseret Book Co., 1976], pp. 48–51.)

Appearance of the Resurrected Lord to the Apostles

Luke 24:36–40

"As they thus spake, Jesus himself stood in the midst of them, and saith unto them, Peace be unto you.

"But they were terrified and affrighted, and supposed that they had seen a spirit.

"And he said unto them, Why are ye troubled? and why do thoughts arise in your hearts?

"Behold my hands and my feet, that it is I myself: handle me, and see; for a spirit hath not flesh and bones, as ye see me have.

"And when he had thus spoken, he shewed them his hands and his feet." (Luke 24:36–40.)

Appearances of the Savior to Latter-day Leaders

Elder Melvin J. Ballard

Away on the Fort Peck Reservation where I was doing missionary work with some of our Brethren, laboring among the Indians, seeking the Lord for light to decide certain matters pertaining to our work there, and receiving a witness from him that we were doing things according to his will, I found myself one evening in the dreams of the night in that

sacred building, the temple. After a season of prayer and rejoicing I was informed that I should have the privilege of entering into one of these rooms, to meet a glorious personage,
and, as I entered the door, I saw, seated on a raised platform,
the most glorious being my eyes have ever beheld or that I
ever conceived existed in all the eternal worlds. As I approached to be introduced, he spoke my name. If I shall live
to be a million years old, I shall never forget that smile. He
took me into his arms and kissed me, pressed me to his
bosom, and blessed me, until the marrow of my bones seemed
to melt! When he had finished, I fell at his feet and, as I
bathed them with my tears and kisses, I saw the prints of the
nails in the feet of the Redeemer of the world. The feeling
that I had in the presence of him who hath all things in his
hands, to have his love, his affection, and his blessings was
such that if I ever can receive that of which I had but a fore-
taste, I would give all that I am, all that I ever hope to be, to
feel what I then felt! (Bryant S. Hinckley, *Sermons and
Missionary Services of Melvin J. Ballard* [Salt Lake City:
Deseret Book Co., 1949], p. 156.)

President Lorenzo Snow (as told by his granddaughter, Allie Young Pond)

One evening when I was visiting Grandpa Snow in his
room in the Salt Lake Temple, I remained until the doorkeep-
ers had gone and the night-watchman had not yet come in, so
Grandpa said he would take me to the main, front entrance
and let me out that way. He got his bunch of keys from his
dresser.

After we left his room and while we were still in the large
corridor, leading into the celestial room, I was walking several
steps ahead of Grandpa when he stopped me, saying: "Wait a
moment, Allie. I want to tell you something. It was right here
that the Lord Jesus appeared to me at the time of the death of
President Woodruff. . . ."

Then Grandpa came a step nearer and held out his left
hand and said: "He stood right here, about three feet above the
floor. It looked as though he stood on a plate of solid gold."

Grandpa told me what a glorious personage the Savior is and described his hands, feet, countenance, and beautiful white robes, all of which were of such a glory of whiteness and brightness that he could hardly gaze upon him.

Then Grandpa came another step nearer me and put his right hand on my head and said: "Now, granddaughter, I want you to remember that this is the testimony of your grandfather, that he told you with his own lips that he actually saw the Savior here in the temple and talked with him face to face." (As quoted in Lewis J. Harmer, *Revelation* [Salt Lake City: Bookcraft, 1957], pp. 119–120.)

Elder Heber C. Kimball

During this time many great and marvelous visions were seen, one of which I will mention which Joseph the Prophet had concerning the Twelve. . . .

He saw the Twelve going forth and they appeared to be in a far distant land. After some time they unexpectedly met together, apparently in great tribulation, their clothes all ragged, and their knees and feet sore. They formed into a circle and all stood with their eyes fixed upon the ground. The Savior appeared and stood in their midst and wept over them, and wanted to show himself to them, but they did not discover him. He (Joseph) saw until they had accomplished their work and arrived at the gate of the celestial city; there Father Adam stood and opened the gate to them, and as they entered he embraced them one by one and kissed them. He then led them to the throne of God, and then the Savior embraced each one of them and kissed them, and crowned each one of them in the presence of God. . . . The impression this vision left on Brother Joseph's mind was of so acute a nature that he never could refrain from weeping while rehearsing it. (N.B. Lundwall, comp., *Temples of the Most High* [reprint, Salt Lake City: Bookcraft, 1993], pp. 25–26.)

Born Again—The Mighty Change of Heart

John 3:3-5

"There was a man of the Pharisees, named Nicodemus, a ruler of the Jews:

"The same came to Jesus by night, and said unto him, Rabbi, we know that thou art a teacher come from God: for no man can do these miracles that thou doest, except God be with him.

"Jesus answered and said unto him, Verily, verily, I say unto thee, Except a man be born again, he cannot see the kingdom of God.

"Nicodemus saith unto him, How can a man be born when he is old? can he enter the second time into his mother's womb, and be born?

"Jesus answered, Verily, verily, I say unto thee, Except a man be born of water and of the Spirit, he cannot enter into the kingdom of God.

"That which is born of the flesh is flesh; and that which is born of the Spirit is spirit.

"Marvel not that I said unto thee, Ye must be born again." (John 3:1-7.)

What It Means to Be Born Again

Elder Theodore M. Burton related the following:

One day, as I was traveling on a plane to New England, I entered into a conversation with a young stewardess sitting in the seat next to me. Most members of our Church know how to steer a conversation toward the gospel, and, before long, we were talking about religion. She told me that she had recently been converted from her former manner of living and was now "saved." I congratulated her. Then she added that she was now a "born-again Christian."

I asked her how she was born again, and she told me that she had accepted Jesus Christ as her personal Savior and now believed in him. I told her how wonderful that was, but explained that acceptance and belief in Jesus Christ is normally called faith. She said, "But I have changed my former way of thinking and living. I am now on the path of eternal life." Again I congratulated her and told her *that* change is normally called repentance. "But," she said, "I have felt a marvelous spiritual change come over me which has purged all evil from my soul." I then asked her if this were not a gift from the Holy Ghost. "I suppose it is," she admitted, "but I mean I've had a *sanctification* experience, not through any work that I or any other person has done for me, but a work of grace whereby Jesus has pardoned my sins and promised me eternal life. I don't need any formal church organization to accomplish this. A person needs only that wonderful, spiritual experience, or feeling of grace." She added that she had truly been reborn spiritually. From her words, I knew she did not understand what is meant by being "born again" nor what is termed the second birth. ("A Born-Again Christian," in *Brigham Young University 1982–83 Fireside and Devotional Speeches* [Provo: University Publications, 1983], p. 35.)

The doctrine of second birth is important to understand. Although they are not a part of the above story, the following prophetic pronouncements will help us better appreciate what Elder Burton was trying to explain to the stewardess.

"The phrase *born again* has a deeper significance than many people attach to it. This changed feeling may be indescribable, but it is real. Happy the person who has truly sensed the uplifting, transforming power that comes from this nearness to the Savior, this kinship to the Living Christ." (David O. McKay, "The Divine Church," *Improvement Era*, June 1962, p. 405.)

"Sins are remitted not in the waters of baptism, as we say in speaking figuratively, but when we receive the Holy Ghost. It is the Holy Spirit of God that erases carnality and brings us into a state of righteousness. We become clean when we actually receive the fellowship and companionship of the Holy Ghost." (Bruce R. McConkie, *New Witness for the Articles of Faith* [Salt Lake City: Deseret Book Co., 1985], p. 290.)

Mere compliance with the formality of the ordinances of baptism and confirmation does not mean that a person has been born again. No one can be born again without baptism, but the immersion in water and the laying on of hands to confer the Holy Ghost do not of themselves guarantee that a person has been or will be born again. The new birth takes place only for those who actually enjoy the gift or companionship of the Holy Ghost, only for those who are fully converted, who have given themselves without restraint to the Lord. Thus Alma addressed himself to his "brethren of the church," and pointedly asked them if they had "spiritually been born of God" and had received the Lord's image in their hearts, which always attends the birth of the Spirit. (See Alma 5: 14–31; see also Bruce R. McConkie, *Mormon Doctrine*, 2nd ed. [Salt Lake City: Bookcraft, 1966], p. 101.)

"You might as well baptize a bag of sand as a man, if not done in view of the remission of sins and getting of the Holy Ghost. Baptism by water is but half a baptism, and is good for nothing without the other half—that is, the baptism of the Holy Ghost." (*Teachings of the Prophet Joseph Smith* [Salt Lake City: Deseret Book Co., 1976], p. 314.)

"Being born again," Joseph said to the Twelve just before they left for England, "comes by the Spirit of God through ordinances" (*Teachings of the Prophet Joseph Smith*, p. 162).

Tell the people to be humble and faithful, and be sure to keep the spirit of the Lord and it will lead them right. Be careful and not turn away the small still voice; it will teach you what to do and where to go; it will yield the fruits of the kingdom. Tell the brethren to keep their hearts open to conviction, so that when the Holy Ghost comes to them, their hearts will be ready to receive it. They can tell the Spirit of the Lord from all other spirits; it will whisper peace and joy to their souls; it will take malice, hatred, strife and all evil from their hearts; and their whole desire will be to do good, bring forth righteousness and build up the kingdom of God. Tell the brethren if they will follow the spirit of the Lord they will go right. Be sure to tell the people to keep the Spirit of the Lord; and if they will, they will find themselves just as they were organized by our Father in Heaven before they came into the world. Our Father in Heaven organized the human family, but they are all disorganized and in great confusion. (Prophet Joseph Smith to President Brigham Young in a dream, *Manuscript History of Brigham Young, 1846–1847* [Salt Lake City: Elden Jay Watson, 1971], pp. 529–530.)

"He Shall Know
of the Doctrine"

John 7:15–18

"And the Jews marvelled, saying, How knoweth this man letters, having never learned?

"Jesus answered them, and said, My doctrine is not mine, but his that sent me.

"If any man will do his will, he shall know of the doctrine, whether it be of God, or whether I speak of myself.

"He that speaketh of himself seeketh his own glory: but he that seeketh his glory that sent him, the same is true, and no unrighteousness is in him." (John 7:15–18.)

Seeking a Manifestation

President David O. McKay said:

I listened as a boy to a testimony regarding the principles of the gospel, the power of the priesthood, the divinity of this work. I heard the admonition that we, too, might get that testimony if we would pray, but somehow I got an idea in youth that we could not get a testimony unless we had some manifestation. I read of the First Vision of the Prophet Joseph Smith, and I knew that he knew what he had received was of God; I heard of elders who had heard voices; I heard my father's testimony of a voice that had come to him declaring the divinity of the mission of the Prophet, and somehow I received the impression that that was the source of all testimony.

I realized in youth that the most precious thing that a man could obtain in this life was a testimony of the divinity of this work. I hungered for it; I felt that if I could get that, all else would indeed seem insignificant. I did not neglect my prayers, but I never felt that my prayer at night would bring that testimony; that was more a prayer for protection, as I look back upon it now, to keep intruders away—really it was more of a selfish prayer—but I always felt that the secret prayer, whether in the room or out in the grove or on the hills, would be the place where that much desired testimony would come.

Accordingly, I have knelt more than once by the service-berry bush, as my saddle horse stood by the side. I remember riding over the hills one afternoon, thinking of these things, and concluded that there in the silence of the hills was the best place to get that testimony. I stopped my horse, threw the reins over his head, and withdrew just a few steps and knelt by the side of a tree.

The air was clear and pure, the sunshine delightful; the verdure of the wild trees and grass and the flowers scented the air; as I recall the incident, all the surroundings come to me anew. I knelt down and with all the fervor of my heart poured out my soul to God and asked him for a testimony of this gospel. I had in mind that there would be some manifestation, that I should receive some transformation that would leave me without doubt.

I arose, mounted my horse, and as he started over the trail I remember rather introspectively searching myself, and involuntarily shaking my head, said to myself, "No, sir, there is no change; I am just the same boy I was before I knelt down." The anticipated manifestation had not come.

Nor was that the only occasion. However, it did come, but not in the way I had anticipated. Even the manifestation of God's power and the presence of his angels came, but when it did come, it was simply a confirmation; it was not the testimony. . . .

But the testimony that this work is divine had come, not through manifestation, great and glorious as it was, but through obedience to God's will, in harmony with Christ's promise, "If any man will do his will, he will know of the doctrine, whether it be of God, or whether I speak of myself." (John 7:17.) ("A Personal Testimony," *Improvement Era*, September 1962, pp. 628–29.)

"Judge Righteous Judgment"

John 7:24

"Judge not according to the appearance, but judge righteous judgment" (John 7:24).

Lesson at the Gas Pump

It had been a good day at the LDS Institute where I taught. The classes went well and the students seemed interested in what I had to say. Let's just say I felt fairly confident about my abilities and life in general. I certainly knew that I had been given many blessings.

While driving home that evening, I glanced down at the dash and noticed the gas gauge was past empty. Luckily for me, a self-serve gas station was just ahead, so I pulled in and began to fill the gas tank. That was a close call! While pumping the gas, I continued reflecting on my blessings.

Then, after a few moments, an old, dilapidated car pulled up at another set of pumps. The fellow driving looked pretty rough, and I began counting my blessings even more. His hair was long; I had nicely trimmed hair. His clothes were tattered and in sad shape; I had on a nice dark suit. "Poor guy," I thought. "He doesn't have a chance in life!"

I finished pumping the gas and walked inside to pay the cashier. As I reached for my wallet, to my dismay, I found that I had a slight problem—I didn't have any money! After checking my pockets—all of them—I told the cashier I'd be right back, that I needed to run to the car to get some money.

I literally tore the car apart searching for loose change—under the floor mats, in the glove box—but nothing. I had no choice but to go back to the cashier and explain that my home was only about a mile and a half away, and that I'd be right back with the money.

To say that I was frustrated and irritated as I walked back toward the building is an understatement. To make things worse, the ragged young man with the battered car passed by me returning to his car and said, "Don't worry about it." I thought, "Same to you, buddy," although I had no idea what he was talking about.

When I got to the cashier and began to explain my predicament, she informed me that the young man had seen what was happening and paid my bill. I couldn't believe it. I quickly ran out the door and over to his car, telling him that I really appreciated what he'd done for me, but that I lived close by and would be right back with the money.

He just smiled and said, "Don't worry about it. I know what it's like to be broke."

I have conjured up a mental picture of what it might be like at the final judgment. . . .

. . . I don't pretend to know the specifics of how the judgment will occur. But when I get a little prideful about all I have been blessed with, or when I find myself judging others who have less or appear unworthy, I remember the important lesson I learned at the gas pump—and I remember just how far I still have to go. (Randall A. Wright, *Latter-day Digest*, January 1993, pp. 63–65.)

"Through the Midst of Them"

John 8:59

"Then took they up stones to cast at him: but Jesus hid himself, and went out of the temple, going through the midst of them, and so passed by" (John 8:59).

Blind the Eyes of Their Enemies

[In the early days of the Church] the spirit of persecution began to manifest itself against us in the neighborhood where Joseph lived, which was commenced by a man of the Methodist persuasion who professed to be a minister of God. And so crafty was he, that he succeeded in influencing Mr. Hale, father-in-law to Joseph, so that he would no longer give him protection, although he had promised to do so.

Brother Joseph intended visiting the Saints at Colesville on Saturday the 21st of August, and on my return, arrangements were made for the brethren and sisters to meet on that day, if possible, without letting our enemies know anything about it. But Brother Joseph was prevented from keeping his engagement on this occasion, but wrote a letter in which he explained the cause of his not coming: the conveyance in which he intended to make the journey did not arrive from "the west;" and the distance was too great to walk. He exhorted the Saints, in a very excellent letter to remain faithful and true to God, and prophesied that the wrath of God should soon overtake their wicked persecutors.

On the 29th, however, Brothers Joseph and Hyrum Smith, and John and David Whitmer came to fill the before-mentioned appointment to hold meetings and to confirm those who had been baptized in June previous. As they well knew the hostilities of our enemies in their quarter, and also knowing it was their duty to visit us, they called upon our Heavenly Father in mighty prayer that He would grant them an opportunity of meeting with us; that He would blind the eyes of their enemies that they might not see, and that on this occasion they might return unmolested. Their prayers were not in vain. A little distance from my house they encountered a large company of men at work upon the public road, among whom were found some of our most bitter enemies who looked earnestly at the brethren but not knowing them, the brethren passed on unmolested.

That evening the Saints assembled together and were confirmed, and partook of the sacrament. We had a happy meeting, having much reason to rejoice in the God of our salvation, and sing hosannas to His Holy name.

Next morning the brethren set out on their return home, and although their enemies had offered a reward to any one who would give information of their arrival at our place, they got clear out of the neighborhood, without the least annoyance, and arrived home in safety. It was not long, however, after the brethren had left us, when the mob began to collect together and threatened and abused us in the most shameful and disgusting manner during the remainder of the day. (Newel Knight, as quoted in *Scraps of Biography* [Salt Lake City: Juvenile Instructor Office, 1883], pp. 63–64.)

Healing the Blind

John 9:1–7

"And as Jesus passed by, he saw a man which was blind from his birth.

"And his disciples asked him, saying, Master, who did sin, this man, or his parents, that he was born blind?

"Jesus answered, Neither hath this man sinned, nor his parents: but that the works of God should be made manifest in him.

"I must work the works of him that sent me, while it is day: the night cometh, when no man can work.

"As long as I am in the world, I am the light of the world.

"When he had thus spoken, he spat on the ground, and made clay of the spittle, and he anointed the eyes of the blind man with the clay,

"And said unto him, Go, wash in the pool of Siloam, (which is by interpretation, Sent.) He went his way therefore, and washed, and came seeing." (John 9:1–7.)

She Could See Them Both

I feel very humble in receiving the chance to bear my testimony along with so many others, for I do have a testimony of the truthfulness of the gospel, and it grows within me day by day, as I am able to see the power of the priesthood manifested among the faithful.

While laboring as a supervising elder in the North Carolina Central District of the Central Atlantic States Mission, I heard of a marvelous healing in Greensboro.

Sister Lillie Jane Stephens, who had been blind for a good many years from some acid she had spilled in her eyes, was home all alone when two elders came to her house tracting. Her husband had warned her never to let in strangers but to keep the screen locked, so that is what she did. The elders finally explained to her that they felt impressed to give her a blessing that could help her, and bring her much happiness if they could come in.

Her fear was overcome, and the elders were allowed to enter her home. They explained to her the scripture, James 5:14, 15, about calling in the elders to pray for the sick, and she requested them to administer to her. She says that all during the prayer she prayed that she would be able to see their faces before they left. While the elder was still sealing the anointing she said she began to see, and before the prayer was over she could see them both.

This story was related to me after she had joined the church. A few months after I had been transferred into the area she had a stroke which was partially paralyzing so that she could barely get around. She called on my companion, Elder Richard T. Lindberg of Salt Lake City, and myself to administer to her. When the prayer was over, she put her arms around us and said her pain was gone. This second manifestation of the power of the priesthood in Sister Stephens' behalf occurred in March 1952. The next time we returned to visit her she demonstrated her agility with a lively dance.

I know that if we will but have faith, through the power of the priesthood miracles may be wrought in this dispensation just as truly as they were in former times. (Hal J. Coburn, as quoted by Dorothy South Hackworth in *The Master's Touch* [Salt Lake City: Bookcraft, 1961], pp. 151–152.)

"I Am
the Good Shepherd"

John 10

Throughout John 10 the Savior referred to himself as the Good Shepherd. An understanding of the ways of the oriental shepherd helps us more fully appreciate the powerful lessons of love that the Savior was teaching.

True shepherds would gather their sheep safely into a sheepfold at night to protect them from predators. These enclosures were usually built of rocks piled high, with only a small opening to serve as the entrance. Authorized entrance was through the door only (see John 10:1–2). At night, the shepherd would lay across the doorway (see John 10:7, 9). There was no other way to get in the sheepfold but through the shepherd.

Often several flocks were brought into the same fold and one shepherd would stand guard at night, allowing the others to go home to rest. The following morning, as they returned and were recognized by the porter or doorkeeper, each would call his sheep and lead them out to pasture (see John 10:2–3). The sheep knew their master and would not follow the voice of strangers (see John 10:4–5).

At times wild animals, driven by hunger, would desperately try to enter the sheepfold. A hireling, who did not own the sheep, might flee. But true shepherds would never desert the flock. Instead, they would defend their charges with their own lives (see John 10:11–13). The true shepherd's chief concern was the well-being of his sheep (see John 21:15–17).

Even his clothing was designed for the benefit and comfort of the sheep. His coat was large and open and normally had a large pocket attached to it suitable for carrying wounded lambs to safety. Isaiah allegorically referred to this pocket when he bore witness of Christ's role as shepherd: "He shall feed his flock like a shepherd: he shall gather the lambs with his arm, and carry them in his bosom, and shall gently lead those that are with young" (Isaiah 40:11).

Christ is the True Shepherd in every respect. The following three accounts help us better understand the beautiful imagery painted by the scriptures of Christ as our caretaker and shepherd. There is no other way to exaltation but through Him. He is not a hireling, but rather stands as the very one who paid the awful price to meet the demands of justice on our behalf. He leads us to the words of eternal life, and his doctrines quench every gnawing thirst and doubt. He loves us more than we can comprehend, and he invites us all to follow Him. "And he that will hear my voice shall be my sheep; and him shall ye receive into the church, and him will I also receive" (Mosiah 26:21).

The Difference Between a Shepherd and a Hireling

As the Teacher showed, a shepherd has free access to the sheep. When they are folded within the enclosure of safety, he enters at the gate; he neither climbs over nor creeps in. He, the owner of the sheep loves them; they know his voice and follow him as he leads from fold to pasture, for he goes before the flock; while the stranger, though he be the herder, they know not; he must needs drive, for he cannot lead. Continuing the allegory, which the recorder speaks of as a parable, Jesus designated Himself as the door to the sheepfold, and made plain that only through Him could the undershepherds rightly enter. True, there were some who sought by avoiding the portal and climbing over the fence to reach the folded flock; but these were robbers, trying to get at the sheep as prey; their selfish and malignant purpose was to kill and carry off.

Changing the figure, Christ proclaimed: "I am the good shepherd." He then further showed, and with eloquent exactness, the difference between a shepherd and a hireling herder. The one has personal interest in and love for his flock, and knows each sheep by name, the other knows them only as a flock, the value of which is gaged by number; to the hireling they are only as so many or so much. While the shepherd is ready to fight in defense of his own, and if necessary even imperil his life for his sheep, the hireling flees when the wolf approaches, leaving the way open for the ravening beast to scatter, rend, and kill.

Never has been written or spoken a stronger arraignment of false pastors, unauthorized teachers, self-seeking hirelings who teach for pelf and divine for dollars, deceivers who pose as shepherds yet avoid the door and climb over "some other way," prophets in the devil's employ, who to achieve their master's purpose, hesitate not to robe themselves in the garments of assumed sanctity, and appear in sheep's clothing, while inwardly they are ravening wolves. (James E. Talmage, *Jesus the Christ*, 3rd ed. [Salt Lake City: The Church of Jesus Christ of Latter-day Saints, 1916], pp. 417–18.)

The Perfect
Law of Love

John 15:9–15

"As the Father hath loved me, so have I loved you: continue ye in my love.

"If ye keep my commandments, ye shall abide in my love; even as I have kept my Father's commandments, and abide in his love.

"These things have I spoken unto you, that my joy might remain in you, and that your joy might be full.

"This is my commandment, That ye love one another, as I have loved you.

"Greater love hath no man than this, that a man lay down his life for his friends.

"Ye are my friends, if ye do whatsoever I command you.

"Henceforth I call you not servants; for the servant knoweth not what his lord doeth: but I have called you friends; for all things that I have heard of my Father I have made known unto you." (John 15:9–15.)

Disappeared Beneath the Water

Our Heavenly Father loved us so much that he gave us his Only Begotten Son, who would atone for our sins and enable us to return to the Father's presence. And Jesus' love for us was so great, he was willing to lay down his life for us. The following story illustrates that kind of love.

On a cold, dark, and overcast Wednesday in Washington, D.C., an airliner was preparing to take off. It was 13 January, 1982. Ice formed on the wings of the jet so quickly that just as it took off, the plane stalled and lumbered back to the ground. Its tail struck a bridge and broke off, and the body of the plane crashed through the ice and sank in the Potomac River.

Within minutes a rescue helicopter was on the way. Only the plane's twisted tail section was protruding from the ice. For a few moments, everything was perfectly still in the icy black water. And then three men and three women managed to surface and cling to the frozen aluminum debris. They were spotted in the swirling snow by the paramedics aboard the helicopter. A rope with a life ring was lowered, and an older man with a moustache and gray hair surrounding his balding head grabbed it. The paramedics watched in amazement as this man handed the rope to the woman next to him. She managed to get into the ring and was taken to shore for safety. Someone threw another ring into the chopper as it started back.

When the helicopter was again over the wreckage, two ropes were lowered. The older man caught the rings and handed them to another woman next to him. She was too weak to hang on. Another younger man grabbed the rings and placed his arms around the two remaining women. A third man grabbed the rope, and the helicopter pulled the foursome through the water to the shore.

Quickly they turned back and hovered over the tail section in the water. But that's all they could see. The man who so selflessly handed the rings to the others had slipped below the water and was gone. He had sacrificed himself so that others might live. How grateful they must still feel for him to this day!

He Will Place His Arms
Unfailing 'Round You

John 20:15–16

"Jesus saith unto her, Woman, why weepest thou? whom seekest thou? She, supposing him to be the gardener, saith unto him, Sir, if thou have borne him hence, tell me where thou hast laid him, and I will take him away.

"Jesus saith unto her, Mary." (John 20:15–16.)

Sisters Who Serve

Faithful women have always responded quickly to the call to serve. "Sister Polly Angel, wife of Truman O. Angel, the church architect, relates that she and a band of sisters were working on the 'veils,' one day, when the prophet and Sidney Rigdon came in. 'Well, sisters,' observed Joseph, 'you are always on hand. Mary was first at the resurrection, and the sisters now are the first to work on the inside of the temple.'" (Edward W. Tullidge, *The Women of Mormondom* [New York: Tullidge and Crandall, 1877], p. 76.)

Just as Mary waited near the tomb of Jesus, centuries later Lydia Knight pondered the death of her husband, Bishop Newel Knight. She worried about caring for her seven children and about responding to Brigham Young's call to move west. Susa Young Gates wrote about Lydia's desperate loneliness:

"How could she . . . prepare herself and family to . . . take a journey a thousand miles into the Rocky Mountains[?] The burden weighed her very spirit down until she cried out in her pain: 'Oh Newel, why hast thou left me!'

"As she spoke, he stood by her side . . . and said: 'Be calm, let not sorrow overcome you. It was necessary that I should go. I was needed behind the vail [sic]. . . . You cannot fully comprehend it now; but the time will come when you shall know why I left you and our little ones. Therefore, dry up your tears. Be patient, I will go before you and protect you in your journeyings. And you and your little ones shall never perish for lack of food.'" (Susa Young Gates, *Lydia Knight's History* [Salt Lake City: Juvenile Instructor Office, 1883], pp. 71–72.)

The Still, Small Voice
of Peace

John 20:19–22

"Then the same day at evening, being the first day of the week, when the doors were shut where the disciples were assembled for fear of the Jews, came Jesus and stood in the midst, and saith unto them, Peace be unto you.

"And when he had so said, he shewed unto them his hands and his side. Then were the disciples glad, when they saw the Lord.

"Then said Jesus to them again, Peace be unto you: as my Father hath sent me, even so send I you.

"And when he had said this, he breathed on them, and saith unto them, Receive ye the Holy Ghost." (John 20:19–22.)

A Mission President's Experience

I will never forget my most memorable, inspirational experience with this principle of listening to the still, small voice. I was representing our Church at a "Religion in Life Week" at the University of Arizona at Tucson. A Jewish rabbi, a Catholic father, a liberal Protestant priest, an orthodox Protestant priest, and a Mormon elder had been invited to represent their various religious faiths and introduce their viewpoints to problems and issues of current interest. This was part of a attempt by the university to bring a religious dimension into the classroom and into the social clubs.

On the second night I was invited to speak at a sorority-fraternity exchange at a sorority house on the subject of "the new morality." The house was packed with about one hundred and fifty young people. They were sitting in the front room, in the dining room, in the hallway, and up the stairs. I had a terrific sense of being overwhelmed and surrounded, and I felt very alone.

The "new morality" is a situational ethic based on the idea that there are no absolute truths and standards but that each situation must be looked at in terms of the people involved as well as other factors that might be present. I put forth my point of view and my conviction that there is a God, that there are absolute truths and standards that have been revealed, and that the "new morality" is merely a rationalized old immorality. I sensed throughout my entire presentation considerable resistance and disbelief. When it came to the question and answer period, two articulate students began to express themselves strongly in favor of this situational ethic of the "new morality." One was particularly effective and persuasive and acknowledged to the entire group that he knew it would be wrong for young people who were unmarried to live together as man and wife; he said that he wasn't advocating any evil thing, but that love is so sacred and so beautiful, if an unmarried man and woman truly and deeply loved each other enough, then premarital relationship would be logical and right.

Though I sensed considerable support for this point of view, I continued to express my beliefs and quoted some scriptures to support them. I sensed there was little faith in my scriptural support, and to many of these students I was pretty much "out of it." I tried to reason that terrible consequences resulted from breaking the law of chastity. The particularly persuasive student on the front row agreed and indicated that the individuals involved were to be careful and responsible and unselfish but certainly not to be prudish. I asked him directly what would happen if a person were to take poison unknowingly. Would it not still bring on terrible consequences? He answered that it was poor analogy; that I wasn't giving enough value to the freedom that genuine love grants.

I remembered praying inwardly for some help and direction, and I came to feel that I should teach the idea of listening to the still, small voice of the Lord, of their conscience. I quoted the scripture earlier mentioned, Revelation 3, and indicated that if they would listen very carefully, they would hear a voice. It wouldn't be audible, and they wouldn't hear it in their ear, but they would hear or feel it deep inside, in their heart. I challenged them to listen, to meditate very quietly, and I gave them the promise that if they would do this, they would hear or feel this voice. Many sneered and jeered at this idea.

I responded to this ridicule by renewing the challenge; I asked each person to try it for himself, and if each person did not hear such a voice in one minute, the group could immediately dismiss me and I wouldn't waste any more of their time. This sobered them, and most appeared willing to experiment. I asked them to be very quiet and to do no talking, but to listen internally and ask themselves, "Is chastity, as it has been explained this evening, a true principle or not?"

The first few seconds some looked around to see who was going to take this business seriously, but within about twenty seconds almost every person was sitting quietly and appeared to be very intent in thinking and listening. Many bowed their heads. After a full minute of this silence, which probably seemed like an eternity to some, I looked at the individual at my left who had been so persuasive and vocal and said to him, "In all honesty, my friend, what did you hear?"

He responded, quietly but directly, "What I heard I did not say."

I turned to another who had been disagreeing and I asked him what he had heard.

He answered, "I do not know—I just don't know. I'm not certain any more."

One fellow stood up spontaneously in the rear. "I want to say something to my fraternity brothers I have never said before. I believe in God." Then he sat down.

A totally different spirit came to that group, a spirit that had distilled gradually and silently during that minute of silence. I believe it was the spirit of the Lord or the spirit of Jesus Christ that they felt inside. It had some interesting effects upon them. For one thing, they became subdued and quiet and rather reverent from then on. For another, it communicated worth to them. They became less intellectual and defensive and more open and teachable. I believe it also met a real need and confirmed some hopes and perhaps convicted others.

It was easy to teach from then on. I felt as if seed was falling on fertile soil. I was enabled to bear witness of the living Christ, the restored gospel of Jesus Christ, and the divinity of the Book of Mormon as concrete evidence of this restoration. I invited many to come out to the Institute of Religion, and later inquiry indicated that they had. I was able to loan some copies of the Book of Mormon. Many stayed around afterward merely to talk about this matter and other spiritual and religious matters. I discussed this experience with an institute teacher the next day and he had almost an identical experience that very night. (Stephen R. Covey, *Spiritual Roots of Human Relations* [Salt Lake City: Deseret Book Co., 1970], pp. 161–63.)

Index